Big Questions

Equipping the church
Engaging the community

ANDREW GOLDSMITH

Scripture quotations are taken from the Holy Bible, New International Version Anglicised Copyright © 1979, 1984, 2011 Biblica. Used by permission of Hodder & Stoughton Ltd, an Hachette UK company. All rights reserved. 'NIV' is a registered trademark of Biblica UK, trademark number 1448790.

Cover photo by grafixart grafixart_photo on Unsplash

© Andrew Goldsmith 2018

All rights reserved.

ISBN: 1986596354
ISBN-13: 978-1986596350

DEDICATION

To James and Anna, who ask great questions, with love.

What people said about this book:

Many times as a church leader I was asked how ordinary Christians without a theology degree could learn to answer their friends' questions about suffering, the evidence for God's existence or the interplay between faith and science. At the time it was not immediately obvious to me what resources I should offer them. This book, however, comes now as a very helpful and comprehensive tool for leaders who want to create space for the kind of conversations where both these ordinary Christians and their friends can begin to get to grips with big questions.

> *Dr Chloe Lynch, Lecturer in Practical Theology, London School of Theology*

Seeing as most people in the UK wouldn't venture over the threshold of our church buildings, *Big Questions* challenges us to go and meet in 3rd spaces to connect people with the very good news of Jesus. A key characteristic of this resource is to go and help people make sense of the Christian faith through tackling the top 5 tough questions that hinder people exploring Christianity.

This is an excellent resource, tried and tested with careful research from years of practice. Andrew has produced a valuable gift for the church to help us actively connect with people in the UK with the most common questions they are asking.

> *Rev. Chris Duffett, Evangelist and Artist, The Light Project*

This brilliant outreach resource is a gift to the church. The five talks offer satisfying answers to the questions of our day and present them in an accessible style.

> Rev Malcolm Hazell, Senior Pastor, Union Baptist Church, High Wycombe

Big Questions is a splendid book, but more than this it provides all the resources to run a Big Questions event. Arising from a very encouraging experience of a number of such events, Andrew Goldsmith has written an accessible, informed and engaging guide to some of the 'big questions' that face those exploring and grappling with Christian faith, making a case for Christianity which is 'good, true, reasonable, compelling and attractive'.

I warmly recommend this book for groups and individuals seeking to deepen their understanding of God and the Christian faith, and for those wanting to put on a Big Questions event.

> Rev Geoff Colmer, Regional Minister and Team Leader, Central Baptist Association

I was thrilled when I first heard about the Big Questions course that Andrew had devised. Following years of running Alpha courses at our church, I had become aware that as fantastic as they had been for Christians or those who had some understanding of God already, it was assuming too much for those who weren't even at that point. We're currently planning our third Big Questions and finding it really helpful in engaging with those who would describe themselves as agnostic or atheist in a way that isn't defensive but enables truth-seeking discussion in a neutral environment.

This book is a brilliant overview of how the course runs and the values that drive it. The talks have also been a good starting point for crafting our own, and I hope others find this course as helpful as we have.

Rev Simon Cragg, Minister, Christchurch, Welwyn Garden City

The conflict between science and faith is a common perception within popular culture. Summarising material from a wide range of sources, Andrew affirms the value of both, helping people to faith to appreciate the value that science brings to our understanding of creation. Whilst not everyone will agree with every point, I commend Andrew for encouraging debate in this important area which I am sure the material will do, helping people to get a bigger understanding of life, faith and the cosmos.

Rev Dr Dave Gregory, Senior Minister, Croxley Green Baptist Church, BUGB President 2018-19. Dave worked previously at the Met Office, European Weather Centre and Hadley Centre on clouds, weather forecasting and climate modelling.

CONTENTS

1	Introduction	1
2	Defend, Explain, Engage	3

What is apologetics?
Why is apologetics important?
Apologetics for the Church
Apologetics in the New Testament
Shaping up for the Big Questions

3	Which Big Questions?	17
4	Setting the tone	23
5	Making it happen	27

The Big Questions

6	Is there a God?	35
7	Science vs. Faith: Is God irrelevant?	59
8	How can a good God allow suffering?	83
9	Is Christianity just a moral myth?	101
10	What is the meaning of life?	123
	Books and Resources	141
	Acknowledgements, About the Author	

Chapter 1

Introduction

The aim of this book is to equip and inspire churches to reach out with the gospel. Jesus commands us to make disciples but we are also told to "go" and do this. *Big Questions* presents one way amongst many to go and connect with people, a resource that hopefully connects with many communities, proves manageable and attractive, expands beyond some familiar comfort zones and, importantly, opens up new conversations about the really good news we have in Jesus Christ.

Big Questions was created as a course by a group of us at Ampthill Baptist Church (Bedfordshire, UK). The initiative has proved very effective, we have run it several times and the course has been picked up and copied or adapted by other churches.

This course does not aim to replace a more straightforward presentation of the Christian message, in the manner of Christianity Explored or the Alpha course, which are truly excellent resources. The church must keep on presenting the gospel as a priority and do so in clear, engaging, attractive and accessible ways. Big Questions has a focus on apologetics, the questions which often precede the topics addressed by these other courses.

We set out to provide a model for engaging the questioning sceptic, the thinking unbeliever, the confused or curious friend who come with genuine questions. These questions look genuinely interesting, can be provocative and hard to respond to, and may be very significant to the spiritual search. We've called them simply the Big Questions.

This book is intended to provide all the resources needed to run your own Big Questions course (though you will need to provide your own speaker, a venue, the guests, and good coffee). It outlines some of our thinking regarding why we would run such a course in the first place, how we shaped it, which values we sought to hold onto, what would be helpful to consider in practical terms if you wish to put on this event, and then the outlines or scripts for the various talks. Also included are discussion starter questions, which we make available each evening of the event to kick-start the discussion after the main talk. Finally, there is a list of books and resources which link to the questions, some of which we had available for guests to borrow or buy, others are listed as resources for speakers as you shape your own talks.

We are very grateful to the team who were involved in this: to ABC for the prayerful support and enthusiasm, and to the staff and management of Costa in Ampthill for serving us and making their venue available to us. We're also thankful for the many guests – over 120 in the first 3 series of Big Questions – who brought their questions and challenges, but also showed interest, openness and honesty in exploring these great big questions.

Chapter 2

Defend, Explain, Engage

What is apologetics?

To defend and proclaim. Apologetics is both on the 'defensive' and the 'offensive' in this sense. It makes the case for a belief or worldview, Christianity in this case, as good, true, reasonable, compelling and attractive. Apologetics often seems quite novel to the new enquirer, in my experience. Many have genuinely not realised or even considered that there might be good reasons for belief in God, or for Christianity specifically. Many approach this area with sincere belief ('faith' even!) that their questions are so monumental, obvious and unanswerable that actually debating them is an odd idea, or a very novel one. Even, as if they are the first person to come up with a particular objection. Yet apologetics is as old as ideas: every idea is open to explanation, defence, opposition, and argument for or against. Christianity is no different in this regard and Christian apologetics is far from new.

Why is apologetics important?

Apologetics is important as a God-given means to engage with people who do not share our Christian faith. To listen to and talk with people who have different views, real questions, perhaps doubts and objections, is helpful in itself. To go on to engage with the ideas and understanding they bring in order to defend Christianity and to positively proclaim and offer it to others is vital and urgent. It engages the world with the Christian worldview, ultimately with the gospel of Jesus Christ.

Christianity is grounded in truth. It is open to robust rational exploration and challenge. It can stand on historical foundations, it is philosophically coherent and rich, and billions of people have found it to be profoundly intellectually satisfying and stimulating, not to mention life-transforming. Apologetics shines light onto all this, as ideas are defended or proclaimed. It has the potential to lead people to a clear, confident faith in Christ – that alone tells us it is very important.

Having run both the Alpha course and Christianity Explored in the past, I could see the real value in these and how they can touch and transform lives. Courses like these are vital tools in a church's hands, and we run such courses in Ampthill, too. Big Questions was aimed at a different group of people and with a different angle. It had in mind those who perhaps would say they have no interest in religion, the church, or Jesus, so would be less likely to come along to Alpha. They would certainly not enter a church building (not that any course has to be run in a church). Often this group (and we've all met them) would raise what they feel is a show-stopper objection to Christianity, what Timothy Keller has called a 'defeater belief', i.e. a belief which seems so blindingly obvious in defeating the notion of Christianity that these people don't *reject* the gospel as they never get near to even *hearing* the gospel. They reject it without hearing it.

Many people in our community who don't belong to a church are not asking the questions which Alpha asks. We might want them to, but they aren't. Many know nothing about Jesus, the Bible, faith or why these are remotely relevant. Many find them mythical, odd, outdated or even dangerous in our modern world – "religion causes wars", etc. Such people don't have the interest or background to want to discuss those 'religious' questions. They may even be put off by the religious nature of a course (what we might consider an evangelistic and Bible-based approach). So we felt that something was needed to try to meet these people where they are, to take a few steps back, addressing preliminary questions which block the way, posed in a manner to attract and engage rather than the explicitly Christian or gospel-shaped questions we might want to be talking about. This was the thinking behind Big Questions.

Apologetics for the Church

The main aim for the Big Questions event has been to engage with those thinking people without faith or searching for faith. Yet there is also great value for the Church. Engaging with the big questions enables Christians to grow in their confidence, to grasp something more of how their faith is reasonable, intellectually coherent and satisfying, indeed very strongly so. Christianity is grounded in historical truth, in evidence, in a variety of rational arguments about origins, meaning, values, destiny and truth. It is not wishful thinking, opinion, fantasy, tradition or, worse, deception.

Apologetics is extremely helpful and important for the Christian in building them up in a more confident and secure faith. It helps the Christian to address questions for themselves, to establish a foundation for why they believe what they believe. It can also be important in sorting the primary questions (e.g. Is God real? Is the Bible trustworthy? Can we know God?) from the secondary questions (e.g. What about tsunamis? How do I make sense of evolution vs. creation? Why does the Church have so many denominations? How do spiritual gifts work?). Once we explore the questions around our faith, we soon discover where the pillars are which support the whole building and we identify the chief cornerstone to the whole construct. Will will then have less anxiety or concern over the more minor aspects of how our faith works out or where the doubts and questions come from – whether our own or those of other people. Apologetics doesn't need to answer every question, but it tends to focus our minds and clarify which questions really matter.

Apologetics also equips the Christian to articulate their faith, to share it, to defend and explain it more fully. None of us has all the answers, and we don't need to. But there are clear and good answers to many of the most common questions and objections. Exploring and hearing these gives us greater confidence and ability to 'always be prepared to give an answer to everyone who asks you to give the reason for the hope that you have' (1 Peter 3:15).

Apologetics in the New Testament

As a very brief means to encourage and inspire our efforts to defend, articulate, explain and proclaim – of which apologetics is a key part – consider some of these examples from the New Testament.

The convincing ministry of Jesus

Jesus performed many miracles which were never merely for show but to lead to faith, to reveal his identity and mission, to underscore his message. In various ways, they provided evidence, reasonable grounds for belief. For example, he said:

> But if I do them, even though you do not believe me, believe the works, that you may know and understand that the Father is in me, and I in the Father. (John 10:38)

> Believe me when I say that I am in the Father and the Father is in me; or at least believe on the evidence of the works themselves. (John 14:11)

He sought to provide evidence, to convince and demonstrate grounds for belief. The faith was not rooted in the miracles, but in who did them, and his revelation of God's kingdom. The very first miracle recorded in John's Gospel led to faith in Jesus:

> What Jesus did here in Cana of Galilee was the first of the signs through which he revealed his glory; and his disciples believed in him. (John 2:11)

The miracles of Jesus prompted faith in him as a person, in his identity, his message and his mission (e.g. John 2:11; 11:25-27). For many, their faith in Jesus Christ, their conviction of who he was and what he could do, led to healing, including healing from leprosy (Luke 17:19, "your faith has made you well"), from blindness (Matthew 9:28-29; Luke 18:42), from demonic powers (Mark 7:28-29), and from bleeding (Mark 5:34). The faith of the friends of the paralysed man leads to his forgiveness from sin and physical healing (Matthew 9:2;

Mark 2:5; Luke 5:20). Faith is a wholehearted trust in Jesus and through his ministry people became convinced and confident enough to trust in him, with life-changing results.

Peter and the other disciples had seen and believed Jesus and his words. They had weighed up evidence, and became convinced of him to the extent that Peter could speak for them all:

> "Lord, to whom shall we go? You have the words of eternal life. We have come to believe and to know that you are the Holy One of God." (John 6:68-69)

After the resurrection, Luke tells us that Jesus sought to convince the disciples through evidence, 'convincing proofs', not merely information or feelings.

> After his suffering, he presented himself to them and gave many convincing proofs that he was alive. He appeared to them over a period of forty days and spoke about the kingdom of God. (Acts 1:3)

This is again the language of evidence and persuasion, and here it is tied closely to proclamation of the good news of God's kingdom. Apologetics and evangelism are overlapping, complementary activities, which we see in the ministry of Jesus and the apostles, and this remains the case for the church now.

The variety of Jesus' apologetics

We also see how Jesus would relate to a wide variety of individuals – men and women, rich and poor, those in power and those with none, the desperate and the proud, the intellectuals and the doubters. Through his encounters we also see how adaptable, flexible, varied his *approach* could be – fitting his questions or challenges to their needs, their concerns, their barriers, and so on. We can learn much from Jesus in this regard.

To Nicodemus, the high-minded and educated religious leader, Jesus gives a rich theological lesson in new birth and of his radical mission (John 3:1-21). He is challenging yet engages with the question. To the Samaritan woman by Jacob's well (John 4:1-26), Jesus is gentle, sympathetic, uses her questions and misunderstandings (or are they attempts to change the topic?) to lead her deeper into the truth and reveal his true identity. To the man by the pool of Bethesda, despite healing him, Jesus is directly confrontational, openly challenging, and ends by issuing a stern warning (John 5:1-15). He would also take opportunities to speak in public in the temple courts (John 7:14) or in more informal settings wherever the opportunity arose (Matthew 5:1; Mark 4:1), as well as in private (Mark 4:10). On trial before Pilate (John 18:33-38), Jesus engaged with the questions asked, even then coming back with more questions (as he did so often), often redefining the terms. To the confused disciples on the road to Emmaus, he still began with their questions and doubts to lead them towards the truth (Luke 24:15-27), offering comfort and reassurance, bringing clarity and hope.

There was not a one-size-fits-all approach to how he explained, proclaimed, defended or argued for his message. This should call us to great sensitivity and listening, but also confidence and liberty in how we take different approaches depending on the question, the person and the context.

The apologetic apostles of Jesus

If we consider the testimony of the apostles we also find a plain and repeated desire to persuade, convince, give evidence, argue for the truth, to lead to faith. Apologetic motivation and activity is not hard to find.

Luke begins his account of the gospel by indicating his evidence as careful, reliable and ordered, intended to bring confidence and certainty regarding the good news:

> With this in mind, since I myself have carefully investigated everything from the beginning, I too decided to write an orderly account for you, most excellent Theophilus, so that you may know the certainty of the things you have been taught.
> (Luke 1:3-4)

The fourth gospel has a summary of John's intent towards the end, rather than in the preface, where he plainly expresses his desire that his testimony about Jesus – the evidence – will lead to saving faith:

> But these are written that you may believe that Jesus is the Messiah, the Son of God, and that by believing you may have life in his name.
> (John 20:31)

The letter of 1 John expresses a similar goal:

> I write these things to you who believe in the name of the Son of God so that you may know that you have eternal life. (1 John 5:13)

The most abundant or prolific apologist for Jesus of the New Testament is the apostle Paul, who is routinely depicted as being in the business of arguing, persuading, teaching not merely in order to win an argument but to present a compelling, urgent and clear case for Christ.

> As was his custom, Paul went into the synagogue, and on three Sabbath days he **reasoned with them** from the Scriptures, **explaining and proving** that the Messiah had to suffer and rise from the dead. "This Jesus I am **proclaiming** to you is the Messiah," he said. Some of the Jews were **persuaded** and joined Paul and Silas, as did a large number of God-fearing Greeks and quite a few prominent women. (Acts 17:2-4)

We find similar activity of reasoning, persuading, arguing to all manner of people elsewhere in his ministry. In Acts 18:4 and 19:8, it is within synagogues; in Acts 17:22-34, Paul addresses pagan philosophers, worshipping 'the unknown God'. Paul is flexible, adaptable, able to relate to his hearers on their terms and within their familiar frame of reference, seeking to make his case to which some respond with belief and some with rejection (e.g. Acts 17:4, 32-34; 28:24).

In Acts 22:1-21, Paul makes his defence to a mob after his arrest, again arguing for his mission, for following Christ. At the very end of Luke's record of Paul's ministry, from house arrest in Rome, Paul continues to seek to declare, explain and persuade:

> They arranged to meet Paul on a certain day, and came in even larger numbers to the place where he was staying. He witnessed to them from morning till evening, explaining about the kingdom of God, and from the Law of Moses and from the Prophets he tried to persuade them about Jesus. Some were convinced by what he said, but others would not believe. (Acts 28:23-24)

Paul's ministry was motivated by a desire for disciples to have a confident, mature faith, with firm convictions of the truth, which is no less than what Christ hopes for his disciples now:

> He is the one we proclaim, admonishing and teaching everyone with all wisdom, so that we may present everyone fully mature in Christ. To this end I strenuously contend with all the energy Christ so powerfully works in me.
> (Colossians 1:28-29, cf. 2 Timothy 1:2; 3:14)

Apologetics has an impact on its hearers, as the gospel is both proclaimed and defended. It can be applied carefully, persuasively, urgently. The obstacles to the gospel can be addressed, as Paul did on Mars Hill or to the crowd at his arrest. The church then and now has been called to this same aspect of our mission, as Peter wrote to the suffering, marginalised church of the first century:

> But in your hearts revere Christ as Lord. Always be prepared to give an answer to everyone who asks you to give the reason for the hope that you have. But do this with gentleness and respect, keeping a clear conscience, so that those who speak maliciously against your good behaviour in Christ may be ashamed of their slander. (1 Peter 3:15-16)

The effectiveness of our defence and proclamation rest on beginning with (and ending with) our commitment to Jesus, our confession of him as Christ our Lord. This underpins our preparation of any answers and the reasons for our hope.

Our methods are to be gentle, respectful, godly and peaceable, so that our manner does nothing to undermine our message. But there is no doubt that the church and every Christian has this calling, and ample opportunity to share what a hope we have.

Shaping up for Big Questions

As well as recognising the value and importance of apologetics, to shape up for a new course meant thinking about who we were hoping to reach.

Many people in the UK are suspicious of Church as an organisation or institution, which means they don't want to come into a church building, much less for a discussion event. They may have had bad experiences of church or simply not feel comfortable in religious services. Sadly, some churches seem oblivious to the need to simply welcome people, greet them, help them find a seat, etc! That should be the easy stuff, long before we get into pastoral situations, getting along with each other, encouraging people in Christian life and holiness and so on, when it can understandably become more challenging. Happily, good experiences of church abound, but that is not everyone's story. The idea of a 'loving church family' may be my happy experience (I'm glad it has been, in numerous churches), but it sounds alien, meaningless or even creepy to many outside the church.

Therefore, a key part of shaping this course was to take an event out into the community, hosting it in a 'neutral' public venue, which would avoid the obstacle of coming into a church building and also enable us to engage very publicly with the community.

We'll cover a range of practical questions in chapter 5, but the venue is key. Hosting an event in a recognised neutral venue makes it easier for the church people to bring their friends. So, for example, we were able to use our local branch of Costa. It's a café, a very nice one, in a building which used to be a bank on the main street through town. It's a stone's throw from the town centre. It is very popular and used by people of every generation, background, religious persuasion and so on. A church can seem to have its own strange 'rules' (where to sit, what to wear, what are the strange things on the wall, when does it start or finish, etc.), before we even start on the religious jargon. Whereas everyone knows the 'rules' of a café: come in, buy a coffee and cake or whatever, sit where you like, talk or be silent, leave when you want. Easy. Running a course in Costa meant our guests already knew exactly what the building was like, where they might sit, what they could drink, and where the door was if they wanted out!

Another aspect of getting ready, of shaping up, was preparing the church to 'go'. Getting out of the church building was significant for our church, to helping ABC grasp something new of mission to our community, reinforcing the sense of mission as serving, witnessing and reaching beyond the church building and beyond Sundays. We are worshippers, disciples and missionaries all the time, everywhere. This gave us a clear opportunity to be that and show that, stretching beyond our comfort zones. We are active in our community in a variety of ways, and intentional about being present and involved, but Big Questions was a brand new idea focused on carrying the message rather than doing good deeds, which is often easier to find the courage for.

When we considered what would be manageable for guests, we opted for a 5-week event. A 10-week course is possible for some but not many, certainly not in our experience, and it might be a deterrent. Five weeks became our standard pattern and has worked well.

So we had the motivation, an idea around clearing the way to hear more about Christianity, a venue, a timescale, and were generating prayerful commitment in the church. We would address some fundamental questions related to Christian faith, at an accessible level, whilst connecting evangelistically with the gospel, the Bible and Jesus Christ. The next question was: which Big Questions should we tackle?

Chapter 3

Which Big Questions?

The themes for the evenings were inspired by various discussions and sources, and by one book in particular which summarised extensive research on modern UK beliefs.[1] Their conclusions were based on interviews with a broad spectrum of people with no religious affiliation, also excluding avowed atheists. They narrowed down the questions which people raised to six main categories:

1. **Destiny**: Where are we going? What is the afterlife?
2. **Purpose**: What's the point of life? What values should I live by?
3. **The Universe**: How did it start? Is it planned? Is it controlled in any way?
4. **God**: Is there a God? Does he/it exist? What is he like? Can he be known?
5. **Spiritual realm**: Is there one? What is it like? Does it have any relevance for (this) life?
6. **Suffering**: Why? Personal, national and international concerns. What can be done?

In our current culture we could decide to consider other questions such as those in relation to other faiths,

---

[1] Croft et al., *Evangelism in a Spiritual Age. Communicating faith in a spiritual age* (Church House Publishing, 2005).

religion and wars, sexuality and gender, truth and trust, nuclear weapons, modern slavery, climate change, and so on. These are all areas where spiritual beliefs and Christian theology in particular has something to say. They would all potentially draw a crowd, stimulate plenty of discussion and offer some answers.

However, it is also important to pause and ask whether a discussion on a topic is likely to help draw someone nearer to a relationship with Jesus by faith, or hinder that movement, or even drive them away. Choosing a topic which is potentially going to lead to fierce disagreements, personal hurt, outright confusion, or is just very peripheral to most people's lives is not going to be productive or foster good relationships with guests. It might end some good friendships!

The five broad topics we chose were: the existence of God; the perceived conflict between science and faith; evil and suffering; the historicity and truth (or trustworthiness) of Christianity; and a final general topic related to spiritual life and meaning.

There is significant overlap between these five topics and the six themes drawn from the research above. This selection of topics gave us scope to draw up five questions which people genuinely ask. We sought to frame the questions in provocative and direct language – the sharp edge of the doubt or disbelief was not blunted or ducked by the question. We felt this was more honest and perhaps made it more enticing. We also addressed the questions in a deliberate order:

1. Is there a God?

We tackled this question first, as this is **the** fundamental question underlying any spiritual searching. It is a question which links to the idea of why we believe anything, to the weighing up of evidence, to what we even mean by spiritual matters, and it is a very accessible and non-threatening topic.

2. Science vs. Faith: is God irrelevant?

Our second topic is one that many find genuinely very interesting. Many have an interest, educational background or some expertise in scientific areas. Some guests may come with a viewpoint on how science fits with faith or suspect it conflicts with religion, or they are just curious to know what to make of it. Some may have heard this topic addressed in some way, but often only through secular media. It has ample scope for illustrations, even live experiments! Science continues to advance. It is routinely in the news, so it is easy to keep the talk fresh with relevant, exciting or fun illustrations. This topic also rarely connects with painful personal experiences in life or with church (unlike the 'suffering' question, or a talk on spiritual life), so we included this as second in the line-up as it was unlikely to put people off from attending the course. This question has always attracted a good crowd and is an obvious one to invite friends or church contacts to who have a scientific background.

3. How can a good God allow suffering?

We don't address this first or second as it is the question which can touch on personal hurts or even tragedies, or a deep sense of God being uncaring, unjust or worse. It is a very common objection or major roadblock to faith, to

Christianity and the Bible in particular, so building a rapport with guests over previous weeks makes sense before addressing this vital question. We genuinely wish to explore the topic and engage with questions, and those questions are often more personal with this topic, hence it comes in third place.

Interestingly, we have typically had our largest turn-out for this topic, as many genuinely want to know "how on earth are you going to answer this question?!" There is a fascination with it, for a few a sense of outrage, and for many it seems like checkmate against Christianity and God being good, wise, powerful or trustworthy.

This topic gives us opportunity to present the message of the cross, the God who suffered, and God's answer and hope in the face of evil.

4. Is Christianity just a moral myth?

We address this next as the most Bible-related talk, so again it makes little sense to include this topic earlier when many guests will have no interest, knowledge or perhaps sympathy for any mention of the Bible. By week 4, the connection between Christianity and the Bible will have been mentioned a few times, although not explored in any great depth. This talk gives us the opportunity to explain the historical evidence for the Bible's reliability, which leads us to highlight Jesus as a historical figure, the historical record of his message and deeds, the historical evidence for his death and especially his resurrection, perhaps referring to the evidence of Christianity's impact on world history and culture, and finally the personal impact – the element of testimony.

5. What is the meaning of life?

Or: Am I wired for a spiritual life?

We have finished the course with a Big Question that addresses spiritual life in some way. This enables us to cover three of the categories identified in the research mentioned above, namely, our destiny, purpose, and the spiritual realm.

This topic gives scope to draw together threads from the previous four sessions and to explore it in its own right. For example, looking back over the first four questions, we can say that there is solid and reasonable evidence for God and indications for what he is like, so what would it mean to relate to him? Given the limits of science yet the indications of design in the universe and ourselves, these hint at our purpose and something more. The suffering question is far harder to handle without a sense of justice, of good and evil, of ultimate purpose – all of which point to something beyond this life, and a desire for ultimate justice, healing, hope. And God knows suffering too. We recap how the historicity and trustworthiness of the Bible underpin Christianity's message of Jesus, who invites people to know and enjoy spiritual life.

Exploring this final question on its own merits also allows us to recognise the very widespread and diverse search for meaning, for spiritual connection, found across all cultures and nations. There are ample stories and examples to draw on. It gives us opportunity to point out the common experience of transcendence, a sense of 'something more', to which spiritual life points. Western atheism can be challenged as relatively novel, strange, and rare in global and historical terms, as well possibly quite dull and dry. There is opportunity to reasonably question what evidence it relies on. In closing, we can again make the case for Jesus as a unique and compelling answer: God in person, evidenced in history, in written testimony and through the testimony of Christians, but who ultimately can only be known be accepting the invitation – faith.

The final talk is indeed very broad. You can choose to emphasise more or less of spiritual practices (e.g. what is prayer, why pray), or insights from other religions or from neuroscience (e.g. does neurology tie in with religious experiences? are some people wired differently for spiritual life?), or to bring in a discussion on comparative religion (e.g. Islam vs. Christianity vs. Hinduism, etc.). How you choose to do this may well depend on local context, on the guests who come, or the knowledge and experience of the speakers you have available. The script in chapter 10 offers just one way in which we have approached this topic.

For all five outlines in chapters 6 to 10, these are examples of talks and provide a considerable range of ideas and plenty of detail. For some contexts, depending on the audience or speaker or time available, these scripts will need to be trimmed down or simplified but the material is here for you to select from and be inspired to develop and adapt.

Chapter 4
Setting the tone

This section is aimed at explaining what the course aims to be in terms of its values and style. It is written in the hope and expectation that anyone wishing to run a Big Questions event of their own called 'Big Questions' will aim to follow these guidelines. The next chapter deals with details of planning and how to make the event happen.

We have an expectation of goodwill and respect towards the ethos of Big Questions and towards Ampthill Baptist Church (ABC) as the originator and creator of the brand. We would show similar goodwill and speak well of other well-known Christian courses, and trust the same goodwill will be shown towards ABC and Big Questions in how it is run or used. These values are outlined below. That said, each church needs to make it fit and work according to their needs and opportunities, their community and friends. Please feel free to bring your own strengths and ideas – they may well be better than ours!

Big Questions is aimed at thinking people with questions about life, God, the universe and possibly religion. It isn't a teaching course on Christian doctrine, although plenty of that lies behind it, and some comes to the front of stage at times. We created this course to help remove obstacles to belief in Jesus, to present a credible Christian answer to these big and tough questions, to offer some direction towards Christ whom we hold to as our own hope and answer, and to show that we are real people who have thought this through and also still have some questions. It is not centred on preaching nor does it refer to the Bible extensively, but it is explicitly Christian in perspective and does relay the central message of the gospel.

With this in mind, we want to offer a **genuine welcome, with respect and openness**, and be honest that we enjoy exploring these things even where Christians may hold different views to the wider culture or other religions. Our strapline on the posters and fliers is 'Enjoy, Explore, Engage'. We are aiming for this, rather than treating guests as debate sparring partners to beat, or students to bring up to speed with more information, or as merely to be there for a good chat over coffee. The questions may have significant weight for our guests, so open and honest engagement really matters.

We feel the following elements to Big Questions are especially important not simply to run Big Questions well but also to keep the integrity of the brand as it becomes used more widely. Copyright of any scripts remains with the original author(s), but you are free to use the materials as provided in this book.

The elements which form part of Big Questions, and we would ask any other church to respect these in how they reproduce Big Questions, include the following:

Values: being welcoming, open to all, aiming for friendly engagement, respectful, hospitality-focused.

Be authentically Christian yet not sermonizing or preachy, not judgemental or dismissive; not ungraciously criticizing people for their views, attacking other views they may hold in unkind ways, or setting up a parody of opposing views to then destroy a 'strawman'. The event should be free to attend, and ideally the church pays the bill at the end (see Chapter 5). Don't over-run, finish when you say you will.

Voice: be lively, informative, positive, fun, respectful, intelligent without being inaccessibly intellectual, culturally relevant, faithful, empathetic.

Content: address genuine big questions, not narrowly Christian, cultural or religious questions; the content of the talks included here may be used with our permission; be intellectually rigorous without being academic; be accurate and fair in depicting opposing views.

Publicity: include 'Big Questions' as the prominent title, and the strapline 'Enjoy, Explore, Engage'; aim for a professional look – sharp, clean, clear, with the title, logo, and strapline prominent, and clearly show who is running the course with contact details (e.g. "hosted by The Local Church", email thechurch@church.org.uk, website, etc.). A professionally produced and printed poster has a much bigger impact than just colourful words on plain A4 paper.

Chapter 5

Making it happen

By now I hope you are motivated and excited to try your own Big Questions event. You have a sense of how useful, attractive and different this might be. You have friends, neighbours and work colleagues in mind who ask those 'awkward' questions, or seem stuck on a question which is blocking the way. You get the values we have tried to aim for – open, respectful, clear, engaging and Christian!

So, how will you do it?

This chapter aims to run through a range of practical aspects for you to consider. They may not all apply to your context, depending on your church, your community, your existing evangelistic events and ministries (Big Questions is not the only means we use to explore faith or share the gospel), your budget or your local venues.

Prayer: Share the idea with the church and begin to pray as the plan takes shape, as people get involved, and as conversations begin with the venue and potential guests. Keep on praying! (see below, *Including the church*)

Team: It helps to involve a core team in the planning, promotion and running of the event, including some of the tasks and responsibilities listed below. It spreads the load, improves the ideas and 'delivery', and encourages the church as more people get involved.

Venue: We approached our local Costa Coffee, who were just a few minutes' walk from the church and very central to our town, to see whether they might be willing to let us use their premises for one evening a week, for 5 weeks, from 7.30 – 9.30pm. They were very willing and opened up for our exclusive use on these evenings. Alternative venues might be a local pub, a curry or pizza restaurant, a sports club, a library or a community centre. Very deliberately, the venue was not in a church, and was somewhere appealing, accessible, comfortable and serving coffee. We booked the venue well in advance and kept them informed with plans and publicity, which happily they were willing to display.

Timing: Each evening event would run from 8 – 9.30pm. The starting time for the 'official welcome', i.e. from the front, or for the talk was not particularly important, given that guests would tend to arrive between 7.45pm and 8.10pm (it is meant to be a relaxed café environment, after all). It then takes time for guests to order drinks and cake, to be served, and find their seats without rushing anyone. An informal start is quite appealing and important, we found almost everyone enjoyed meeting one another and chatting beforehand. A clear and punctual end point is also appealing and important, for the sake of the guests, babysitters and the café staff.

Dates: We aimed for a 5-week run in a school half-term, or 3 evenings before the half-term and two afterwards. Breaking for half-term did not seem to impact numbers at all. We tend to run the course in the autumn term as the evenings are cold and dark which makes the literally warm welcome all the more appealing. The lead up to Christmas with the opportunity to invite guests to carol services, etc. was also helpful.

Day: This might sound quite trivial – which weekday to go for. But we found that Thursdays were significantly easier for people to accommodate in relation to the working week and the school week (e.g. homework or teaching prep are in the bag by then). It has that 'nearly the weekend' feel. Each town/church/community may have its own rhythm, and the venue availability might decide this one.

Costs: We were ready to pay a fee to hire the venue but none was required, as we anticipated generating more than adequate income for the venue through sales of hot drinks and cakes. We achieved this, but with other providers some 'underwriting' of the cost might be necessary. We give each guest a printed 'voucher' for one free coffee and cake per evening (a distinctive A6 flier with the topic of the evening, the logo, "Welcome", and 'This voucher entitles you to a free drink and cake of your choice."). They could have more if they wish, but the next round is on them. The event is therefore free to guests. At the end of the evening, we paid the bill, which the church covered.

Format: In broad terms, we went for: welcome, coffee, talk, informal discussion in groups.

We toyed with ideas of including live music (see below) and a hot meal, but this adds time, logistics, cost and may put off people from the less 'risky' feel of simply coffee and chat. We deliberately chose not to include opportunity for Q&A, i.e. questions from the floor to the speaker, as this becomes more formal, easily becomes adversarial and would hinder less confident, articulate or argumentative(!) people from speaking. Discussion around the tables with people you know and with just a few others is far easier and more relaxing for most guests.

Running order: Each evening would run as follows:

7.40pm: our team arrive and check-in with venue staff. We rearrange some furniture, set up a microphone, amp and lectern. We put up Big Questions posters, leave fliers on tables and layout a 'bookstall' near the entrance. We're also there before the guests so we can welcome them and chat as they arrive.

8.00pm: guests have started to arrive, we gently encourage them to order drinks, etc. so we don't have a huge queue at 8.15 (it takes time to serve 30+ cappuccinos, hot chocolates, mochafrappa-cortadillerichios, etc.). Guests gradually take their seats.

8.10pm (approximately, check the queue first): one of the team gives a welcome from the front, explains the aim of the event, highlights our desire to 'enjoy, explore, engage' with no strings attached and our openness to questions, then very briefly announces the topic for the evening and introduces the speaker.

8.15pm: a 25-30 minute talk on the Big Question for the evening. Conclude with thanks, then invite them to discuss.

8.45pm: 45 minutes for discussion in groups around the tables. We supply some 'starter questions' but have never found it needs much prompting to generate discussion. These questions are designed to provide a prompt or reminder at times, rather than an agenda to work through. The team tend to sit at different tables and join in, depending on who we know or who is not already part of a group. We aim to keep discussion going but not to lead in a very strongly directive way.

9.30pm: one of the team takes the mic and thanks people for coming; we begin clearing up.

9.35pm: leave promptly, so staff can do a final clean and clear-up.

Equipment: We used a small portable amplifier, a microphone with cable and stand, and a music stand as a portable lectern for the speaker's notes.

Background music: It was really helpful to have some background music, only turning it off for the talk itself. Most cafés have their own soundtrack and can control the volume. If they don't have this, bring a smartphone and speaker, and choose your own playlist.[2]

People: Each evening would need a speaker, one or two others to facilitate discussion, a welcomer or two, a musician if live music is included, and hopefully people bringing guests! It is a whole church who make this effective (see below).

Music: Consider whether live music would be a draw or a distraction. This depends on the talents you have available, how practical this might be in the venue, and the space and acoustics. It wasn't right for us but might be for you.

---

[2] Which could be a lot of fun in itself, linking the songs to the Big Question of the evening.

Advertising: Don't underestimate the impact of posters, postcards in local shops/cafes, promotion via the church website, etc. Email your entire congregation with a PDF flyer to forward to friends. Ask to use public noticeboards, send a copy to local newsletters or magazines. Ask the venue to promote it. Go for quality production, not just simply a Word document on white A4 paper, as it will stand out. Find someone in the church gifted in graphic design. (You can check our church website for examples of our graphics.)

Speakers: Where possible, have a team of speakers. This spreads the load and more importantly it brings a variety of perspectives, voices, personalities and styles. It allows scope to develop some gifts too. For the science talk, it can be helpful if the speaker has some scientific credentials, for example. Bear in mind that this is definitely not preaching and is quite distinctly different to preaching; someone may be an excellent preacher but may not be comfortable or clear when handling this kind of topic and style. Someone else may be brilliant at presenting science from a faith perspective, or a philosophical approach to spirituality with lively cultural examples, but completely ill-equipped or unsuited to preach. But also be confident in the people God provides: we have good answers to the questions and in any speaker we don't need a polished professionalism or an epic speech. We need clarity, humility, some humour, empathy, some personal testimony, and a natural means to point to the gospel, to Jesus.

Bookstall and resources: We offered a range of books for guests to browse or buy, or just take if they could not afford them (see chapter 11). Depending on timing, e.g. approaching Christmas or Easter, some simple booklets or tracts might be appropriate as would publicity about church events, services, courses, etc.

Including the church: Big Questions will not appeal to everyone nor be accessible to every member of the church, given family or work commitments, health or age. It will capture the imagination of many though and it needs the prayerful support and encouragement of a whole church. We provide regular reminders and promotion within church services in advance of the start date, both to invite people and to prompt the church to invite and pray. The church building and mid-week groups are also used to publicise it (and we promote it via the website, notice sheets, noticeboards, facebook, etc.). Nearer the time we set aside particular times to pray and include this during the course – in church services or by prayer emails. Where possible we have had a group meeting to pray at church during the event. We also aim to keep the church informed of how it is going, which is only polite as we're all paying for the coffees!

Follow-up: We deliberately did not ask for contact details. We relied on personal invites for most guests, so there was an existing link for follow-up. We gave a clear invitation to the church events, services, groups and so on. The church building is only a few minutes' walk from the café and very well-known in the town. Our contact details and website were on all the publicity. We took this approach as we wanted it to have a light touch, not any sense of recruitment. We did not want to abuse people's openness to spiritual matters or their respect for Jesus thereby fuelling any suspicion or antipathy to the idea of church. We found the existing networks of friendships were adequate for establishing ongoing contact. In terms of follow-up events, apart from

Christmas/Easter highlights as a church, we have seen people join our mid-week youth groups, seniors lunch events, come along on Sundays, or attend an Alpha course. Others have been followed up pastorally, even over coffee in Costa.

...

There is no one set way to run Big Questions. Hopefully, the elements of the event listed here can help you plan, prepare and spark further creativity to make it as attractive, interesting and engaging as possible.

In the following chapters we have included scripts for each of the 5 Big Questions. These are our scripts and each speaker can shape their own, with each audience and context in mind. Bring in the local or contemporary stories, anecdotes and news events as appropriate, as well as personal testimony and timely humour. These are provided to offer ideas, inspiration and a starting point. This is not meant to be the final word on each Big Question.

Chapter 6

Is there a God?

The Very Short Version
The material here covers a lot of ground and you might want to keep to this script or pick and choose for a shorter talk. The outline of our talk is as follows:

Acknowledge the question as being very common and significant, give examples, help define the question. Present four main arguments for God's existence:

- Evidence from **the existence of the universe** (cosmological argument).
- Evidence from **the fine-tuning of the universe**, the world, and the existence of complex biological information (teleological argument).
- Evidence from **our sense of moral awareness**, of right and wrong, of moral boundaries even if these vary (moral argument).
- Evidence from **personal experience of Christianity**, the reality of lives changed and culture shaped through Christianity.

...

This is a *great* question to ask and one that has been asked throughout human history. It is far from new, and that fact should tell us that it should not or cannot be easily dismissed.

An article in the *Times* newspaper in October 2014 ran under the headline 'More people believe in aliens than in God.' Who are we talking about though?

Various entries were offered to the book 'Who's Who' to describe God. Here are two examples:

> **GOD (first entry)**; aka Yahweh; Jehovah; The Word; Supreme, omnipresent Being, followed and revered by most of this world's people over centuries; said to have created the world, the universe, man and woman; two s. Absent from all above creations/children; whereabouts unknown. *Residences:* Heaven, the Vatican, Mecca, Jerusalem. *Publications:* Bible, Quran. *Recreations:* hide and seek, devil tormenting, plagues, pestilence, floods, earthquakes.
>
> *See also Adam; Jesus Christ*
>
> **GOD (second entry)**; fictitious character (1143BC to 1951AD); appears in many ancient texts; declared dead in 1950s due to failure to appear at son's birthday; still revered by disillusioned people with no ability to act for themselves who think "prayer" to this God is answer to all man's ills. *Resides:* in minds of men.
>
> *See also Tooth fairy; Santa Claus*

A YouGov poll in 1983 found that 31% of British adults said they had no religion; by 2016, it was almost half.[3] In our society, the UK census data also tells us that there is a rise of the 'nones': those who, when asked about their religion, simply tick the box marked 'none'. Alongside Christians, Muslims, Jews, Sikhs, Hindus, and some of the

---

[3] https://yougov.co.uk/news/2016/03/26/o-we-of-little-faith/

various sects and cults like Scientology, Jehovah's Witnesses, Jedi Knights and so on, there are those with no view, no interest, no god at all.

How can we tell? Do the 'nones' have some insight here? Are they right?

You see, this question actually matters.

> 'Two possibilities exist,' Arthur C. Clarke once wrote, 'either we are alone in the universe or we are not. Both are equally terrifying.'

If there is a God, it matters a great deal what he is like (if we can call him a 'he' for the sake of simplicity). It matters whether he is good or evil, kind or cruel, intelligent or stupid, present or absent, powerful or weak, relational or hostile. There are no rules or laws which must apply to God, as by definition God or gods are outside our world and our laws. That's part of being god-like!

It matters whether there is a God, as we would have to face the consequences of such a Being existing, and our response. Every religion with a god assumes some degree of present and future relational connection, sometimes rewards or punishments. If God exists, knowing that is important, and knowing what he is like is also vital.

But whether you think this question is important probably already depends on what you think this God might be like. Assuming, for a moment, that we agreed the evidence pointed to God existing, it would be quite odd to think he or it had nothing to do with the here and now, no interest in us. Like a vacant Father Christmas character who dispensed goodies but with no day to day role.

But what if there is no God?

Bertrand Russell: 'There is darkness without and when I die there will be darkness within. There is no splendour, no vastness anywhere, only triviality for a moment and then nothing.'

Many in the West would go along with Bertrand on this: life is here, then ... nothing. Not many elsewhere in the world would believe that, but in the UK certainly quite a few. But for those who assert "God doesn't exist", I'd be interested to know how and why anyone has reached that conclusion. What is the evidence for that statement? Where is the *evidence* that there is no god? Whichever way you go on this question, it makes sense to weigh up the evidence, not just go with the crowd. And merely to be indifferent is a curious place to land on, given that either way it has an impact on what life is really all about.

Before we go looking for God, it's worth noting that **not** believing in a god of some kind is relatively unusual in historical terms – throughout history this has been the norm – and in global, cultural terms too. Everywhere else, religious belief and experience is prevalent and has been the 'norm'; parts of the secular Western world are the exception rather than the rule. The spiritual longings of the human heart, a sense of transcendence – of something beyond the material and visible – are common to *all* cultures throughout *all* of history. That's a fact. We might say they are all wrong, but without the evidence perhaps we should be slower to judge.

Some would come back by pointing out that there are so

many versions of 'god', which god might it be? There certainly are various ideas of what a god or 'superbeing' or spiritual reality might be. But to argue that because there are lots of different ideas for god on the table, they must all be wrong, simply doesn't follow. Again it comes down to evidence, and thinking, weighing up what makes sense and what we can know.

We're not going to go into 'which God is it', because the topic tonight is that real starting point – is there even a God *at all*. We're going to explore some of the clearest arguments there are for the existence, the reality of God.

Many people approach the 'God question' thinking "surely that's a matter of faith, not of evidence or argument". As if religion deals in feelings and faith, and leaves arguments and evidence to the scientists and rationalists. Come along next week to hear the science stuff!

But we're not talking about a battle between rational understanding and some kind of 'blind faith'. The Oxford professor and scientist, Richard Dawkins has taken a swipe at faith, comparing it to belief in the Tooth Fairy. Yet real faith, the faith Christians talk about, the faith the Bible refers to, is based on evidence, understanding and trust, backed by growing experience. This faith shapes our will, moves us into action and involves our intellect and conscience. Real faith believes because of the evidence, not in spite of it. That is all a long way from blind or misguided mystical "faith", and has an impact beyond mere feelings. 'Blind faith' is not faith as Christians understand it, nor most other religions. Real faith, a wholehearted belief like Christian faith, is something you *grow up into*, not *grow out of*, as we do with belief in the Tooth Fairy or Father Christmas.

Dawkins is a clever man, but offers plenty of rhetoric and noise against religion, not evidence or argument. He doesn't take the question seriously or the evidence.

But how can we know? "**Prove it!**" is the commonly heard cry in response to the question of God's existence. Yet not everything that is true and real *is* provable, as if you could set up a scientific experiment to demonstrate that God exists. If it were that easy, someone would have done it long ago.

- You *can* prove 2 + 2 = 4, that water boils at 100 degrees C.

- You *can't* prove that slavery is unjust, that fascism is a bad idea, why a piece of music can make you cry, or that you are loved.

Does that mean these things are imaginary, unreal, unimportant, or must be false? Of course not.

Not all knowledge is 'provable' by equations and experiments. Our eyes, experience, mind, heart and conscience tell us things we can't *prove* but clearly *know*. Christianity is very much grounded in evidence, as we'll explore in different ways over the next few weeks. It is not a blind faith, but rather based on reasonable trust, growing in understanding, based on historical and intellectual evidence and inquiry as well as personal experience. And it's robust enough for us to explore and challenge thoroughly.

So let's explore the evidence for God. We'll consider just four of the main arguments:

Firstly,

The cosmological argument

The starting point is simply this: **the existence of the universe.**[4]

There is a universe. There is something, rather than nothing. Assuming this is not all completely unreal, a result of an illusion, of random neurological inputs (but are *they* real?), then we accept that we live in a real universe. Even if it is an illusion, why *this* illusion? And why is it so good, so beautiful, so ordered?

We take this for granted usually without stopping to ask: why? Why something, not nothing? We expect a reason for everything else, everything within the universe, so why stop short of asking "why?" of the ultimate 'thing', i.e. everything we can see, the universe? The legendary cosmologist Stephen Hawking was right on target:

> The usual approach of science of constructing a mathematical model cannot answer the questions of why there should be a universe for the model to describe. Why does the universe go to all the bother of existing? Is the unified theory [the Grand Theory of Everything] so compelling that it brings about its own existence? Or does it need a Creator, and, if so, does he have any other effect on the universe?'[5]

The universe is not self-explanatory.

Hawking suggested that the universe could have

---

[4] John Lennox, *God's Undertaker: Has Science Buried God?* (Lion, 2007), 62-3.
[5] Lennox, *God's Undertaker*, 63.

spontaneously appeared, all by itself, because the laws of physics demand it. But this is a simple category error: the laws of physics aren't some objective reality with a power of their own to create anything, they are simply a way of describing how the universe works. The universe reveals these laws, it wasn't created by them.[6]

Even if we follow the notion of multiverses, that there are many or even infinite universes, the fact remains that we are in *this* one. And it begs an explanation.

Thomas Aquinas, the brilliant and influential theologian of the 13th Century, drew on the idea from the Greek philosopher Aristotle of causality – a primary cause which leads to all other causes and events.[7] This same concept of 'first cause' underlies the cosmological argument, traditionally associated with Aquinas.

The argument points to the universe, i.e. the cosmos, and considers its origins. Aquinas sought to lay out a rational statement for the Christian faith and particularly for God's existence. He presented five 'ways' each of which 'points' to the existence of the creator, describing how the world reveals the Creator's 'signature'.

In other words, everything in this world has a cause – a car does not just 'appear', nor does a coffee or a cake. So why is the cosmos any different? Why should we think it just 'is'?

---

[6] See John Lennox, *God and Stephen Hawking: Whose Design is it Anyway?* (Lion, 2011).
[7] Aquinas focused on the example of the Bible and how we understand it, with God as the principal and divine author of the Word, the primary cause, but with human authors as instrumental causes in producing the Scriptures, so the intentions of both parties require our consideration when we are interpreting it.

Aquinas' first Way considered the existence of motion and change in the world. It is a dynamic universe. Science tells us that the universe is expanding and appears to do so from a fixed point in time and space (which also suggests a beginning). Aquinas said that every effect requires a cause, which was evidence for a *first* cause. By stepping back from the universe now, through all the small causes of change, movement and energy, this 'chain' of causality must have a starting point. Tracking the changes seen in the universe back through the series of causes, Aquinas concludes:

> 'We are therefore bound to arrive at a first cause of change which is not changed by anything, and everyone understands that this is God.'[8]

Clearly not everyone 'understands that this is God', either in the 13th Century or now! The main criticisms have suggested a universe without beginning (an infinite regression or series of changes), or a cause that is not God, or many gods; or some unknown superpower, or the 'beginning without a cause' (e.g. from the Scottish philosopher David Hume). But where is the *evidence* for these theories?

Consider the Big Bang theory as an example: if one accepts this as the beginning, it could be asked what caused it? It has to be a cause of immeasurable power, outside of the realm of both space and time (which began at the Big Bang), and able to produce not simply energetic chaos but this hyper-complex and *ordered* reality we now inhabit. Call that power what you like, but there is something. Something powerful, immaterial, timeless, purposeful, complex. **God-like**.

---

[8] Alister McGrath, *Christian Theology. An Introduction*, 3rd ed. (Oxford: Blackwell Publishing, 2001), 248.

Science has been unable to pin down the first cause; by definition, it is beyond our scope to measure. The Bible simply states that the created order bears witness to the Creator.[9] This first argument boils down to this: the universe *is*. It had a beginning. So who or what 'began' it? Who put the 'B' in the Bang?

Let's look at the second argument:

The teleological argument

Isn't it kind of handy that we have an atmosphere that is breathable? And that food grows in the ground (and such varied food)? And trees and plants do such a good job of scrubbing the carbon dioxide out of the atmosphere and pumping out oxygen – that is *really* convenient. The sun is close enough to warm us, even to enjoy, not so close it incinerates all life. And as for us, *homo sapiens*, we're quite amazing in many ways – our immune system fights zillions of enemies every day, our brain handles quadrillions of requests better than any email server, we're endlessly creative (some of it in good ways), and we have not yet destroyed the planet. All of this should surprise us daily!

The second argument for God's existence picks up on this and highlights that sense of *design or fine-tuning* in the universe and the world. The incredible statistical unlikelihood of life existing *at all*, never mind such complex, diverse and beautiful life, suggests that it cannot be by chance.

It goes by the classy name of the *teleological* argument, which states that the universe and its constituent parts show evidence of design with a purpose, or of being

---

[9] Psalm 19:1-2; Romans 1:21; Acts 14:17.

directed towards some goal (or in Greek, *teleos*). This evidence indicates the existence of a designer. Mr Aquinas had this at number 5 in his set of Five Ways:

> There is therefore an intelligent being by whom all natural things are directed to their end. This we call "God".[10]

Imagine you decide to go out for the day with some friends or family and head off to a stately home. When you've picked up your guide book and map, the kids quiz and treasure hunt, clocked where the loos and the ice cream stall are, you head off into the grounds. Behind the magnificent house, you step out onto the immense stone veranda overlooking the ornate gardens. And what a sight they are! There are fountains dotted around the place, a myriad of colours and sizes of flower beds arranged to draw your eye down the lines and pick out the contours of the land, gaps for pathways bring you to various statues and quirky sculptures or deliver the best panoramic vistas, with benches tucked away in alcoves in the hedge – which itself is like a work of art with animals carved into it. Beyond that, the perfectly neat lawns which are regular shapes but cleverly laid out to create a sense of movement away from the grand house. As you stand there, do you think, "Wow, what a cool garden, and to think this just emerged by itself out of the mud!"?

No. I would suggest you are more likely to think, "Wow, that is cool, that is stunning, and how skilled, how visionary is the gardener who turned a beautiful idea into a reality!"

When we look at ourselves, our world, our universe, we

---

[10] McGrath, *Christian Theology*, 250.

might well be wowed by the complexity and scale (we are so small, it is so big), or by its endless beauty and diversity (just watch *Blue Planet*, or visit the local park). But when we look closely, a reasonable answer is not "wow, this just ... exists", like a garden that came from nowhere, but "wow, this was made for us."

A classic outline of this argument was developed by the English theologian and natural philosopher William Paley in the 18th Century. He was fascinated by the work of Isaac Newton and his discoveries of the cyclical and regular aspects of nature, from which the variety of mechanical sciences still draw. Paley saw the machinery of the Industrial Revolution as a metaphor for the larger, more complex mechanism of Newton's universe, and suggested that any mechanism involved 'contrivance': design for a purpose, not simply ordered. Just as a watch, clock or machine could not emerge by purposeless chance but required intelligent, purposeful design, Paley argued that nature is a mechanism, too. He pointed to the manifestations of design within the physical and biological world, far greater than in any machine, as evidence of an intelligent Designer.

To illustrate, Paley described a situation where a working, ticking watch was found lying in a field. Various theories could be constructed to explain its structure, workings and origin, such as the interaction of physical forces – wind, rain, ice, pressure, etc. – but none of these theories were as likely as the existence of an intelligent, purposeful designer.

David Hume was the most prominent critic, questioning whether it was valid to extrapolate from observing order in the world to argue for a designer and that being to be God. He criticised Paley's comparison of the world with a watch, which was clearly designed, whereas a living organism, such as a plant, could simply grow and not require design. Hume suggested that in the vastness of the universe and time, an ordered world such as ours could occur by 'random' chance. Evolution – the processes of natural adaptation and selection – draws on this idea.

However, these criticisms still fail to adequately address the *philosophical* question of where the *first* designs came from (our cosmological argument) – how does a plant know how to grow like that, much less a human being? What is the origin of the information needed to govern plant growth or cell development? Or the *scientific* question: how has such incredible diversity evolved and so rapidly? We cannot dismiss the possibility of God as the most likely source of this fundamental information – the designer in chief. The beauty and intricacy of design in nature remains beguiling and demands a good answer.

Let me just give you a sense of the complexity and unlikeliness of our world and universe, which we will explore further when we look at science and faith.

Many years ago I studied engineering. One of my lecturers explained the famous second law of thermodynamics this way: when you slide down the bannister, your bottom gets warmer; as your posterior cools down, you do not slide back up the bannister. Energy tends to dissipate – it's called entropy. Another way of putting it is that things tend towards disorder, the quantity called entropy always tends to increase on the large scale. The probability of the universe having a sufficiently *low* form of entropy initially, to allow the ordered universe we have now which permits life, rather than a *high* entropy universe (one that is an energetic, formless chaos), has been calculated as 1 part in 10^{123}. 10 with 123 zeroes following it. This number is so vast, it is more than the total number of particles in the universe. 1 in 10^{123} is a fantastically, incomprehensibly, *small* probability.[11] Yet here we are, alive, in this universe.

And there is quite a list of similar 'magic numbers' for this apparently fine-tuned universe. Scores of physical properties of the universe which, if they were tweaked by an infinitesimal amount either way, would render human life or indeed any life impossible. As if it were planned that way.

The alternative explanations come up against problems too. Life from nothing towards a living cell is impossible by evolution (evolution can only work on something already alive), nor is the range of species explicable, nor can mutations explain the development or evolution from one species to another – rabbits can get faster but within limits; they don't become cheetahs![12]

It's not just the complexity which is a major problem for the 'pure chance' or evolutionary theory. The universe *simply isn't old enough* to explain the level of complexity we see, either. Evolution hasn't had long enough, even if we think it was capable in the first place. For evolution to work it would need a chief monkey (to use Dawkins' example) to organise it. It would need to know where it is going, what it needs to achieve and identify the key mutations needed to meet that target.

There's a further consideration if we look at how 'fine-

---

[11] Lennox, *God's Undertaker*, 69-70.
[12] Edgar Andrews, *Who Made God? Searching for a theory of everything* (Evangelical Press, 2009), 216-220.

tuned' or well suited this universe is to life, to human life, to organic life. And it's also a further problem for the 'pure chance' argument: *information*. For example, take one strand of human DNA. This construct has 3 billion base pairs in each cell, which fits into a space just 6 microns across (0.006mm). It's tiny. But if you stretched the DNA in *one cell* all the way out, it would be about 2m long. Take all the DNA in *all* your cells and stretch it into a line, and it would be about twice the diameter of the Solar System.[13] And that is one *long* piece of *information*. Yet information can't 'emerge' or 'evolve', even to programme a coffee machine, much less a zillion miles of human DNA to programme you or me. It needs external input. Where did all this coherent, specific, complex information come from?

To give you a different picture of the complexity of human beings, consider these findings from a study of computing power:

'In 2007, all the general-purpose computers in the world computed 6.4×10^{18} instructions per second. [That number is] ... in the same general order of magnitude as the number of nerve impulses executed by a single human brain. Doing these instructions by hand would take 2,200 times the period since the Big Bang.

Looking at both digital memory and analogue devices, the researchers calculate that humankind is able to store at least 295 exabytes of information (a number with 20 zeroes in it.) Put another way, if a single star is a bit of information, that's a galaxy of information for every person in the world. That's 315 times the number of grains of sand in the

---

[13] www.sciencefocus.com/qa/how-long-your-dna

world. But it's still less than one percent of the information that is stored in the DNA molecules of a [single] human being.'[14]

We are, quite clearly, amazing.

Complexity can occur, but *information* – organised data with meaning – can't simply evolve. How could it? It's not merely improbable, it's impossible. We'll look at the complexity of life more in the next session, 'Science vs. Faith'.

Science is phenomenal and wonderful when it comes to the question of 'what' and 'how', but it can't begin to answer questions of 'why' or 'who' – of purpose, intent, meaning, personal engagement. These categories are beyond it. Yet our universe, our planet, has glaringly obvious indicators of purpose, intent, meaning. It has God's fingerprints all over it, if we are looking carefully at the evidence.

The world we live in is astonishingly diverse, beautiful, majestic even, and sits under a canopy of stars and space that we have only just begun to explore. Where did it come from? How is it so beautiful? Why do we notice that – what makes us capable of discerning order and beauty?

This argument falls short of proof, but most things in life do! However, it's a compelling argument for God's existence – evidence awaiting your verdict.

---

[14] Extract from Martin Hilbert and Priscila López, '*The World's Technological Capacity to Store, Communicate, and Compute Information*', Science, 10 February 2011.

The third argument relates to each of us:

The moral argument

This is what has been called the moral argument. We each have a sense of right and wrong, of good and evil. We have an idea of what is just. We are aware of our own guilt at times. But why? Where does this moral awareness come from?

The moral argument stems from observations of human behaviour. Although the actual meaning of what is 'good' or 'right', for example, may vary by country, culture and era, this awareness is common to all. Historically, it is also well sustained. There is a universal experience of a sense of right, wrong, obligation and conscience; an objective awareness of what constitutes 'good' behaviour or 'truth'.

Once again, Thomas Aquinas was ahead of the game and this was his Fourth Way. From his examination of human values such as goodness and truth he set this out as evidence of God.

The moral argument states that the only rational source of our moral nature is a morally good God, the original transcendent cause or standard of what is good and true. But you might ask: why can't *we* decide what is good and true? Surely it doesn't have to be a 'God answer' at all.

Perhaps we just need to "follow our hearts", go with what seems best, and try to do no harm to anyone else. But what if our hearts are corrupt? The greatest command of Christianity is to 'love God and love your neighbour'. In remote parts of the world, where cannibalism was practiced, "following your heart" turned out to mean '*eat* your neighbour', not love them. Were they wrong? They were only "following their heart"!

Or how do we judge those who commit ethnic cleansing? Or the criminal minds behind the Holocaust? Or serial killers? Or paedophiles? Or Islamic State terrorists? All examples of individuals following their own deep-seated beliefs, their 'hearts', yet we would rightly agree they are depraved, wrong, wicked. We might even describe them as evil.

But how do we know? Where does this moral judgement come from?

Some have pointed to sociological factors as the source of this behaviour, with God as a construct we've invented to support our notion of good and evil. But that does not answer where society at large derives such consistent values. Whether or not people recognise God as the source of 'the moral law', the moral argument raises this important question.[15]

We know we live in a moral universe. We are moral beings. Every child grows up knowing how to be naughty! Why? How? Who said this universe *should* have a moral code?! Physical laws, evolution and neuroscience can't explain this. It all points to a moral agent, a force or being who makes us live and think this way, whom many call God.

Without a fundamental, objective moral being then all actions become relative and this can lead to any number of horrific outcomes as Nazi Germany, ISIS and others show.

---

[15] Romans 2:15

The fourth and final argument is quite different again:

Personal experience of Christianity

I can't prove to you that God exists, just as no one can prove that he doesn't. But what we can do is look at the evidence. So far, I've given you a feel for the evidence and argument based on the universe existing, then we've considered the evidence of how complex and purpose-made it all is, then briefly the moral argument – our moral judgements and questions only make sense if there is a moral standard outside ourselves, and this points us to God.

The fourth argument is more personal. It rests on faith, experience and history. You can still test the evidence, but there are different kinds of evidence.

For me, as for many others around the world and throughout history, the evidence for God is connected to personal faith and personal experience. And for me, these in turn rest on two pillars: **the trustworthy, historical evidence** (which we look at in week 4 of Big Questions, 'Is Christianity just a moral myth?'), and **the experience of knowing the person of Jesus himself**. Both are based on evidence, not merely feelings, ideas or opinions.

The *historical* evidence is rooted in what actually happened in history, centred on the story of Jesus of Nazareth and his life and death. If he is God in person, that matters a lot. I'm just going to leave that for today, as we'll come back to that in week 4.

Let's spend a few moments as we come to a close thinking about the argument from *experience*, from changed lives.

The argument from experience is seen in the evidence of changed lives for billions of people. It's there, for example, in the motivation to serve others, especially the poor, the untouchables, the most vulnerable, around the world. I'm not for a moment saying that being kind is somehow unique to Christians at all (and Christians can be unkind, thoughtless, selfish and so on at times), or religious people in general, but wherever Christianity has emerged across all cultures it has provoked movements of positive and often radical change: the readiness to serve the poor, to protect the weak, to work for education and healthcare, to advance the rights of women, children and those with disabilities, to end slavery, to promote justice, to advance the rule of law, to develop rights for women and the disabled, to preserve life, to overthrow apartheid and oppression.

Christianity has *founded* many of these ideals and *shaped* all of them. For all its failings (which are caused by human beings, not the teaching or person of Jesus Christ), Christianity has a legacy of changed lives.

It doesn't prove God. But the individual lives and the history of modern civilisation shaped by this Jesus movement are evidence we can't dismiss easily.

Then there are the individual stories of what it means to know God. Those who describe him in terms of a personal trust, dependence, love, friendship. The experience of knowing forgiveness and a fresh start. Those who find from him resources for life: wisdom, hope, peace. I could tell you my story of what it means to know Jesus, to be a Christian. That's basically what being a Christian is – knowing Jesus, having a living and active faith, a spiritual life with real hope, real forgiveness, new peace and purpose, all because of him. I can't prove that with an equation, I can tell you it's real.

You can question these beliefs, even the sanity of such people! But the evidence is still there, of lives and even nations changed for the better.

It's real, it works, it changes lives.

Summary

These four arguments are all quite logical and clear. They're not fake news or merely noisy opinions. They cannot prove God in an objective sense and none is above criticism. But you can't simply dismiss them. Weigh up the evidence.

The Bible itself does not set out to prove God nor does it lay out any such proof, yet it reveals the clear conviction throughout, as a backdrop to the narrative, that *God is*.

Given the weight of these arguments as a whole, I would suggest that it is actually harder to believe that there *isn't* a God. If we don't believe that there is a God, we are left finding other reasons to explain something out of nothing, the incredible reality of complex intelligent life in a 'fine-tuned' universe, the basis of our morality, the prevalence and life-changing power of faith, and our sense of 'something out there'. Science can *describe* some of these things, it can't *explain* any of them adequately.

And the Christian experience itself: the story grounded in history of the man called Jesus of Nazareth. The claims of that story only make sense if he were not merely a man but God in person. That experience of knowing him lives on today in billions of people who have not left their brains at the door, erased their deductive reasoning or joined a cult. They've not blindly accepted tradition, but found Christianity to be true and effective, because *God is*.

I hope this has given you a different way of looking at things and food for thought. Over to you!

Discussion starter questions

1. Does the term 'God' have positive or negative connotations for you? Would the world would be better off with (or without) such a being?

2. Do you think a day will come when humanity will 'grow out' of it's need for religious belief? Why or why not?

3. What do *you* think caused the universe to come into being?

4. Is there anything in nature that you would say looks like it has been 'designed'? Is it reasonable or ridiculous to say that design could suggest a designer?

5. Why do you think altruism exists? Why do we feel we should care for the vulnerable? Do such feelings come from God or something else?

Chapter 7

Science vs. Faith: is God irrelevant?

_____

The Very Short Version
The material here covers a lot of ground and you might want to keep to this script or pick and choose for a shorter talk. The outline of our talk is as follows:

- Identify **the assumption that science is ultimate**, it can answer everything, that religion is useless by comparison.
- **What is faith or belief?** Like science, it relies on evidence, not wishful thinking or fairy tales.
- **The value of science**.
- **The false conflict myth**: science and faith can enrich and illuminate each other.
- **Science in place of God**: the dangers of science, its limited scope, it is never complete.
- **What science tells us about the universe**: seven 'signposts' pointing beyond science (the origin, existence and intelligibility of the universe; the fine-tuning for life of the universe and planet Earth; the existence of information and of irreducible complexity).
- **Science points beyond itself**: the need for other 'maps' of reality to answer life's ultimate questions, and faith as an important, powerful, meaningful map.

...

When you hear 'science versus faith', perhaps you're thinking 'evolution vs. creation', or maybe 'rational people verses religious people'. Or the search for the 'God particle'? This subject is much bigger and richer than those topics, which can just end up generating more 'heat' than 'light' and not get us very far. Exploring science versus faith can be really rewarding.[16]

This topic is an important one as it is a timeless topic. There will always be new scientific discoveries and many will evoke wonder at the universe in its complexity and beauty. Science is a means of celebrating the ingenuity and creativity of the human race, and Christianity would happily go along with that, too.

However, scientific discoveries are sometimes presented as if the following were true:

- *firstly*, that science is increasingly answering all of life's ultimate questions and will one day do so exhaustively; and

- *secondly*, that science (and scientists) have a power to explain things to which religion and people of faith have little or nothing to add by comparison; the two camps are portrayed to be increasingly at odds with science providing more 'useful' answers compared to religion which is of questionable value.

Does that sound familiar? "Science will answer everything" and "religion is useless next to science"? Is **God** irrelevant?

We'll look at questions like these tonight: is science the ultimate last word? Or, do faith and science *both* have a role in the face of life's greatest questions and needs?

---

[16] This talk can have various titles. We used *Science and Faith: is God dead?* and *Science vs. Faith: is God irrelevant?*

The aim of this talk is not to attempt the last word on this topic, it's a big question in more ways than one. I do want us to explore how science and faith relate and see what each brings to exploring life, the universe, meaning and indeed everything, and see how science leads us to ask but can't answer the ultimate questions.

There is no one, single, perfect way to answer this Big Question. One size will not fit all, nor is this the comprehensive answer as *we* are all different, *science* is always changing, the *world* is too, and faith is not itself a science!

As we've mentioned faith, let's clarify what that means. You might have come across Richard Dawkins' bizarre definition of faith, that no serious Christian would recognise: faith "means blind trust, in the absence of evidence, even in the teeth of evidence."[17] He doesn't give any evidence for how he reached this!

Contrast this with how an Anglican theologian described faith:

> '[Faith] affects the whole of man's nature. It commences with the conviction of the mind based on adequate evidence; it continues in the confidence of the heart or emotions based on conviction, and it is crowned in the consent of the will, by means of which the conviction and confidence are expressed in conduct.'[18]

A living, wholehearted faith is not just an opinion nor merely intellectually agreeing with something. It affects

---

[17] Alister McGrath, *Dawkins' God. Genes, Memes, and the Meaning of Life* (Blackwell, 2005), 85.
[18] W. H. Griffith-Thomas, cited in McGrath, *Dawkins' God*, 86.

your whole being and living – your mind, conscience, actions, intellect, values, and so on. It's an act of trust based on evidence, not a blind faith at all. Science and faith both rest on *evidence*.

The value of science

Science can be quite literally amazing. Without it, life would be greatly impoverished. It has the ability to astonish us, revealing aspects of our universe or ourselves which are breath-taking and beautiful (or sometimes plain weird). Newton's laws of motion have incredible predictive power to describe our everyday world of apples falling from trees, planes flying, cricket balls heading over mid-wicket, combustion engines and much more besides. Einstein's theory of relativity extended that even further, to infinity and beyond. The Hubble telescope brings us amazing images of remote galaxies. *Blue Planet* revealed life nearer to home, in all its bewildering beauty (and cruelty at times).

Science enables us to predict, describe and understand our universe from the sub-atomic level of quantum physics to the distant stars, with endless discoveries along the spectrum between those extremes. Science (and maths) are incredibly powerful at describing things, telling us how things work or fit together.

Science *is* awesome. But it lacks *explanatory* power. It can't tell us "why?" If someone bakes a cake, science can identify the ingredients and calorie count. It can't tell you that you're loved and it's your birthday. It can't tell you what love means, either.

Science can also find itself caught up in controversy on ethical issues: embryonic stem cell research, nuclear weapons proliferation, human cloning. But is the problem not with science, but with religion? Is 'faith' the enemy of science? Let's look at that a bit more closely.

The false conflict myth

For some there is the idea that to be a Christian (or follow a religion) you might need to switch off your brain, park it at the door. Maybe Christians are a bit dim? Just as a simple experiment (which is itself a scientific thing to do), I counted the number of people in my local church who have a PhD in science or engineering. Out of perhaps 160 adults regularly involved, there were 8 with doctorates.[19] That's quite a few in any church. Two of them are professors. None of them appear to be psychologically disturbed or show any distress or discomfort at all with being – at one and the same time – professing Christians and highly qualified in scientific subjects. And they are not unusual. Not in this way, anyway.

And that shouldn't surprise us. Religious belief, and Christianity in particular, is entirely unrelated to a person's scientific achievement or general educational level. A young child can be a Christian and have a real, vibrant and clear faith, albeit at a child-like level. Similarly, someone with profound learning disabilities can have a genuine Christian faith. Or the most eminent Nobel prize-winning scientist can fail to grasp what faith is. Knowledge and faith don't perfectly correlate, otherwise would only a genius be confident of being a Christian?

---

[19] And a PhD is only one measure, of course. As for wisdom, that can't be measured in qualifications.

So you can be a Christian regardless of scientific ability or understanding. Being a scientist, or approving of science, has no bearing on faith either way.

If we look at surveys of eminent scientists throughout history we would reach the same conclusion. Some of history's greatest scientists were motivated by faith (e.g. the likes of Pascal, Newton, Kepler, Faraday, Babbage, Marconi, Heisenberg, and so on). As a matter of historical fact, the very existence of the modern sciences stems from the Judeo-Christian understanding of the world. The Royal Society, the world's oldest independent scientific academy, was established in 1662 and it founder members were predominantly Christians motivated by their faith. However, many of history's other greatest scientists have been atheists, or agnostic, or indifferent to faith. Scientific endeavour sits very comfortably with the 'God question' but doesn't prove it either way.

For many, their faith didn't just 'fit in' with their scientific convictions and knowledge, it inspired and motivated their pursuit of and commitment to science.[20] Science can be seen to *support* faith, to *align with* a faith-based worldview rather than be in conflict with it. Christianity is not merely intellectual, but it is not less than that. It merits real thoughtful examination, as science does too.

The conflict idea is certainly very popular and has been around a long time.[21,22] The marvellously colourful quotes of Dawkins and company rely on this assumption, and the ugly, even ferocious rhetoric certainly adds their

---

[20] E.g. see *Test of Faith* in the Resources chapter, and Ruth Bancewicz, *God in the Lab: How science enhances faith* (Monarch, 2015).
[21] Wilkinson, in Denis Alexander (ed.), *Can we be sure about anything? Science, faith and postmodernism* (Apollos, 2005), 221.
[22] McGrath, *Dawkins' God*, 139-146.

personal conflict to the equation. However, historians of science have comprehensively shown that this conflict is *a historical myth*. It's a myth based more on social circumstances or political forces in the Victorian era than specific ideas. One historian dismissed this myth as follows:

> 'the idea that the natural sciences and religion have been permanently at war with each other is now no longer taken seriously by any historian of science. It is generally accepted that the "warfare" model was developed by religiously alienated individuals in the nineteenth century to help the professional group of natural scientists to break free from ecclesiastical control – a major issue in the intellectual life of Victorian England.'[23]

In other words, the conflict was about politics, not the truth or value of religion or science. This conflict myth is outdated, wrong, and well past its sell-by date.

In fact, there is a growing interest in how the two disciplines of science and theology (or faith) can have *positive* and *constructive* dialogue, how they can inform and illuminate one another, as well as a growing awareness of the nature of science and its limits.

For those who oppose religion or faith, the root issue is typically not a commitment to science nor proof of any kind but what lies beneath: their worldview and assumptions. If one assumes that 'what we see is all there is' (i.e. a naturalistic, materialistic worldview), then by definition God does not exist or is not necessary. Religion then becomes an oddity and unscientific, or antiscientific.

---

[23] McGrath, *Dawkins' God*, 142.

The myth of science versus religion is tied to this other conflict of a clash of worldviews – not between science and religion but between a naturalistic worldview, the view that nature and what we observe is all there is, and a religious or theistic worldview. There are scientists on both sides.

But let's suppose for a minute though that God *is* dead, and we look to science instead for all the answers. How well does science stack up in the role of a god?

Science in place of god

- ***The dangers of science***[24]

Science is capable of great good – healthcare breakthroughs, vaccines, prolonging life, connecting our world in communication. But it is also capable of great abuse – Zyklon B in the Nazi's concentration camps, napalm, nuclear weapons, nerve agents, computer viruses, the dark web. Human progress is a myth, history proves this again and again. We advance in technology, not in our nature. But the abuse of an *idea* (science or religion, atheism or Christianity) can't discredit whether it is valid or true or not.

Is science itself the problem? No, it is moral choices which are the problem, just like any other human wrongdoing. Just because you *can* do something does not mean you *should*. Science can be a means to great harm and evil, not merely good. We might well say the same of religion. Both religion and science can go bad, kill and destroy.

---

[24] Alister McGrath, *Inventing the Universe, Why we can't stop talking about science, faith and God* (Hodder and Stoughton, 2016), 130-139, discusses when science and religion go wrong.

On that score, science doesn't do well if we treat it like a god.

Secondly, we can't treat science as a god as it is plainly limited:

- **The limits of science**

Sir Peter Medawar, a British biologist and Nobel prize winner, also a Christian, puts it plainly:

> 'The existence of a limit to science is, however, made clear by its inability to answer childlike elementary questions having to do with first and last things – questions such as "How did everything begin?" "What are we all here for?" "What is the point of living?" It is incapable of answering many of the most important and fundamental questions of human existence.'

He noted that science cannot answer these ultimate questions, and no conceivable advance of science would empower it to answer them. He judged that if we are left with faith in science alone, and no answer to life's purpose, it leaves people 'empty and dissatisfied'.[25]

Science cannot explain everything. In fact, it cannot *explain* anything, rather it seeks to *describe* the world. It cannot explain why the world exists, why it is intelligible and has laws at all, or how and why life emerged. Science can't shape or inform our moral vision – what is good, true or just. It has to be shaped by our moral vision, so we need to ask where that comes from.

A telescope can reveal the beauty of the stars. A

---

[25] McGrath, *Inventing the Universe*, 150.

microscope can examine the cells which make up life and our bodies. Neither can tell us anything about why we are here, who to vote for, which GCSEs to choose, what makes us happy, or why we start wars.

Science is limited. It is limited to what is observable or measurable in nature, with no scope beyond that. This does not make anything beyond the measurable *irrational*. Belief in God cannot be proven but it is not irrational. Nor is something false just because it is unproven. It is just that, unproven.[26] You can't measure love or justice but they are still vital, real and rational.

Scientism, the elevation of science as though it can answer everything, is an exercise in over-reaching the limits of science. It's a delusion.

Thirdly,

- **Science is tentative, it is not the final word**

Consider what you *can* actually prove and what you can't. Most things of value in life can't be proved (love, beauty, justice, meaning). Science can tell us *how* the gas chambers of Auschwitz worked; it can't tell us *why* the Holocaust was evil, although we know it absolutely was. Science can't tell us who to marry, whether capitalism is better than fascism, what kind of music we like, where to go on holiday, why we feel loved. Are these unimportant, just because science is completely incapable of answering them? Of course not.

But even the answers science *does* give are tentative and provisional. Conclusions develop, new discoveries make us ditch the old data and models. Science is not an

---

[26] McGrath, *Dawkins' God*, 88.

absolute or total truth. It has given us an increasingly clear view of our understanding of the universe (e.g. the work of Galileo, Newton, Einstein, Hawking), but there is more to come.

Some have the notion that since science is continuing to develop and new discoveries are made, surely it will answer all the questions. For now, the gaps in knowledge or questions we can't answer are temporary, and "God" is just a convenient label to cover these gaps – a kind of 'God of the gaps' argument. This assumes that God has nothing to do with any current scientific knowledge or understanding and that science genuinely can extend to answer all questions – treating science like a god. These two assumptions lack evidence or scientific grounds, it is a worldview rather than sound science.

However, as science and technology have developed, many areas of interest previously thought to be well understood by science have been found to require further explanation beyond naturalistic means. For example, the 'goo' of cell protoplasm was previously thought to be just that – goo. Now it is known to be information-rich biological material, which material processes and evolutionary theory cannot adequately explain. In human DNA, what was once described as 'junk DNA' with no coding information has been radically re-evaluated as a 'jungle' of information. Where did the information come from? Science does not have all the answers

Science is still wonderful and valuable but being tentative and constantly changing we can't treat it like God. It is not all-powerful or all-knowing, indeed such a position would be the antithesis of science – it would be anti-science. Scientific beliefs change.

'Science takes things apart, so we can see how they work. Religion puts them together so we can see what they mean.' Alister McGrath

There is a role for both science and faith.

Science does however have some remarkable lessons for us about the nature of the world we live in. It has wonderful descriptive and predictive power. As we do science, we should notice some very remarkable things about the universe and life in general, as science points to something beyond itself.

What science tells us of the universe

Let's consider seven lessons from science about our universe.

1) The origin of the universe[27]

Did it have a beginning, or has it always been here? Is it eternal ('it just is')? Aristotle and Plato thought the universe to be eternal, but from centuries earlier the Hebrew thought was of linear time, with a Creator God. From the Middle Ages to the 19th Century, an eternal universe was the dominant idea, whereas now in modern science and cosmology particularly, belief in a beginning is the view of the overwhelming majority. The evidence of red shift from distant galaxies (an expanding universe), of cosmic background radiation (pointing to a space-time singularity, the 'echo of the beginning'), and the law of thermodynamics (increasing disorder but from some initial ordered state) all point, on *scientific* grounds, towards a beginning. This is in addition to the obvious philosophical, logical argument that a 'beginning' to

---

[27] Lennox, *God's Undertaker*, 64-8.

everything is easier to contemplate than an eternal universe which 'just is', without a first cause.[28]

Some within the scientific community reject the notion of a beginning, not on scientific grounds but rather because this raises the tricky issue of who or what was responsible. John Lennox points out the great irony of this in our day:

> 'in the sixteenth century some people resisted advances in science because they seemed to *threaten belief in God*; whereas in the twentieth century scientific ideas of a beginning have been resisted because they threatened to *increase the plausibility of belief in God.*'[29]

Science simply cannot answer the question of the origin of everything. By definition, that's outside of the scope of the observable and measurable, of the material world. This origin points towards something or someone existing beyond time, but however close to the 'B' in the Big Bang we might reach by measurement or mathematical model, we cannot cross the horizon of the beginning of space-time with these tools. The Christian faith provides a reasonable answer which fits the scientific data.[30]

---

[28] Keith Ward, *Why there almost certainly is a God: Doubting Dawkins* (Lion, 2008), 51f. A timeless, eternal Being (God) is a far better explanation than any alternative, including the argument of a 'multiverse'. This proposes that all potential universes exist at the same time, including this one, so each universe is 'necessarily existing', and therefore does not need a cause. This is weak on logic and lacking any evidence. It also fails to explain or answer our reflections on this universe.
[29] Lennox, *God's Undertaker*, 66. (italics mine)
[30] William Lane Craig, 'Beyond the Big Bang', provides a very thorough review of the science of cosmology and the related philosophical background to this debate, see www.bethinking.org

Secondly,

2) The existence of the universe [31]

It is there. We have a visible, real universe. It exists. We can touch, feel, taste, hear, enjoy, experience it. There is something, rather than nothing. Science is constantly surprising and rewarding in helping us to describe the universe, to understand its properties and behaviour, but can't begin to tell us 'why?'

The universe is not self-explanatory. We need another set of tools, another way of seeing the world to explain or understand its existence or purpose.

3) It is intelligible

The planets orbit our sun, there are various natural laws (gravity being the most obvious). The universe is so 'regular' – it has a predictability to it, events are repeatable.[32] It is rationally possible to investigate it on the basis of its regular behaviour (orbits, cycles, sunrise to sunset, 'laws', and so on). It did not have to be that way, but it is. We've simply got used to it.

It is from the Judeo-Christian worldview – that the world is created by a personal, intelligent Being – that science has derived its most fundamental assumption: that the world is intelligible and hence can be investigated meaningfully. The belief in such a God also makes such an enterprise as scientific enquiry more than just possible but truly worthwhile, as science explores the handiwork of the Creator. For Christians, it can be worship.

---

[31] Lennox, *God's Undertaker*, 62-3.
[32] See Lucas, 'A biblical basis for the scientific enterprise', in Alexander et al., *Can we be sure about anything?*, 53.

In the words of Kepler, the great mathematician, science is like us 'thinking God's thoughts after him'.

We expect the regularity and repeatability of the laws of nature. This is not just a foundation *for* science but a repeated conclusion *from* science, how the material world from the grand scale of cosmology (the stars) to the virtually invisible scale of quantum physics can be explored, modelled, predicted precisely because it is ordered. But why should this be the case? Why *should* there be such relatively simple laws to describe phenomena such as planetary motion, gravity, electrical resistance and the like?[33] For many mathematicians and scientists, it is precisely the beauty, simplicity and predictive power of these laws that has affirmed their faith in a God who stands behind them. Francis Collins calls mathematics the 'language of God'. It all begs an explanation beyond science.

The universe had a beginning, it exists, it is intelligible and predictable. We learn these from science, but science is limited in explaining any of these. And there's more.

4) It is phenomenally fine-tuned for life

We touched on this in week 1, thinking about God's existence. Various branches of modern physics, and notably cosmology, continue to affirm how remarkably 'fine-tuned' the universe appears to be such that it is capable of sustaining life and how our planet is suited to

---

[33] It has also been noted that it is remarkable that our planet should have such a set of circumstances that allows us to observe the universe at all, i.e. we are near a star, with a visible moon, with observable planets, with clear vision beyond to the stars. This is not the case on countless trillions of other lumps of rock in the universe with opaque atmospheres or remote locations.

our life-forms. Let me share a few examples which get more and more 'unlikely' as we go down the list:

> The energy levels of various atoms (helium, beryllium) in their 'ground state' need to be within a certain range, or there would not be enough carbon to sustain life. A variation in this ratio by **1%** and life would be unsustainable. But that's just odds of 1 in 100.[34]

> If within atomic structures 'the ratio of the nuclear strong force to the electromagnetic force had been different by one part in **10^{16}**, no stars could have formed.'[35] That's odds of 1 in 10,000 million, million.

> If the ratio of the electromagnetic force constant to the gravitational force constant were increased by one part in **10^{40}** (an absurdly, unimaginably small amount) then only small stars can exist; decrease it by the same amount and there will only be large stars. Both large and small stars are needed for a life-sustaining universe: the large to produce sufficient elements and the small to burn slow enough that life can emerge and not be incinerated as the stars burn out. How *infinitesimally delicate* this fine-tuned balance is! It is comparable to (1) a marksman hitting a target 20 billion light years away; or (2) if America were covered with stacks of coins, in piles reaching to the moon (a height of 236,000 miles), and this exercise then repeated on a *billion* similar size continents, then just one coin replaced with a similar coin of a different colour, the probability that a blindfolded person could pick it out is a 1 in 10^{40} chance. The world existing as it

---

[34] You could use some visual aids to represent the numbers in this section.
[35] Lennox, *God's Undertaker*, 69.

does, by chance, through random development, is astonishingly unlikely.

> Or go back to The Beginning: if the ratio of the expansion to contraction forces in the instant immediately after the origin of the universe (the first 10^{-43} seconds) were varied by one part in **10^{55}**, expansion would have been too rapid for galaxies to form, or too slow and the universe would have collapsed. 1 in 10 million, trillion, trillion, trillion.

One last example:

> Entropy always increases, energy dissipates: your coffee cools down, bedrooms naturally get untidy, washing up never ends, and disorder tends to increase on the large scale too (the universe). The probability of having a sufficiently low form of entropy at The Beginning, to allow the ordered universe we now have which permits life, rather than a high entropy universe (of energetic, formless chaos), has been calculated as 1 part in **10^{123}**. This number is *so* vast, more than the total number of particles in the universe; 1 part in that is unimaginably small.

And **all** of these have to be right, not just one, for life to exist. These few examples illustrate the point that the universe as a whole has the overwhelming impression of having been designed or made, to be 'fit for purpose'. It exhibits an astonishing, exquisite balance of multiple parameters which permit life. Science is not able to answer the question 'why', but it is precisely *from* science that we are led to ask this question.

The world-renowned physicist and mathematician, Freeman Dyson said the following:

'the more I examine the universe and study the details of its architecture, the more evidence I find that the universe in some sense must have known that we were coming.'[36]

5) Fine tuning of planet Earth for human life [37]

A fifth lesson from science: it is not just the cosmos, the universe, which gives the impression of fine-tuning. Closer to home, planet Earth also reinforces this evidence:

- ➢ The distance from the Earth to the sun: too hot and all the water would evaporate, too cold and no life could survive. A change of 2% would render life unsustainable.

- ➢ Surface gravity and the temperature on Earth: these need to be within a few percent for the atmosphere, the mixture of gases, to enable life.

- ➢ The angle of the Earth's axis and rotational speed: too fast and winds would scour the surface and prohibit all life, too slow and the temperature range would be extreme.

The probability of one such planet existing in the universe is perhaps roughly 1 in **10^{30}**. Science points to this fine-tuning, and leaves us looking for an explanation.

Two more lessons from science about our world:

6) It is full of information

Information, meaningful data, can't simply evolve. You can't jump from non-life to life. Letters don't become words on a page without an author. A building is not

---

[36] McGrath, *Inventing the Universe*, 81.
[37] Lennox, *God's Undertaker*, 70.

simply a pile of stones but the result of creative, purposeful intelligence. Our bodies, our cells, are shaped by our DNA – our programme, the base information. This code shapes each one of us differently.

One of the greatest scientific discoveries of the modern age is that of the structure of DNA, and that same discovery points to the bewildering complexity of the human genome and the statistical improbability of life emerging by chance.[38] It is a fantasy to think that such complex life 'evolved', it is simply stupendously improbable. Even if complexity can emerge (as if data could organise itself), the age of the Earth is too short to explain the complexity we see. And, of course, we are more than just data.

And last but not least:

7) It is incredibly complex, yet we can't reduce that complexity 'all the way down'. Irreducible complexity exists.[39]

Molecular biology continues to uncover the vast complexity of the living world towards the other end of the spectrum from the stars and the edges of the universe, on the scale of living cells. (Quantum physics looks at an even smaller scale.) A bacterial cell, weighing less than a trillionth of a gram, contains thousands of intricately co-ordinated molecular parts like a machine or factory, comprising some 100 thousand million atoms.

The science which leads us to explore such complexity also brings us to the problem or question of 'irreducible complexity': at this extremely small scale we find

---

[38] Lennox, *God's Undertaker*, 120, provides further examples and data.
[39] Lennox, *God's Undertaker*, 117.

incredible sophistication, co-ordinated structures, which are bewilderingly complex. However, in many instances of such 'molecular machines', if one such part were removed the whole would cease to function. An everyday analogy would be a mousetrap – it *only* works with *all* the parts. Therefore, such a 'machine' could not have evolved or 'emerged' from continuous development into this complex state. This is its 'starting point', it is *irreducibly complex*. It has all the hallmarks not of evolution, nor relying on the laws of nature, chance or necessity, but of design, of intelligence, of purpose. [40]

British professor of philosophy, Antony Flew who for years was an outspoken atheist came to this conclusion later in life:

'A super-intelligence is the only good explanation for the origin of life and the complexity of nature.'

Models and theories of molecular evolution have no answer and certainly no data to explain where this complexity comes from. The answer lies elsewhere.

In so many ways, science highlights our need for explanations beyond science.

---

[40] Lennox, *God's Undertaker*, 118. Michael Behe gives the intriguing example of 'the tiny acid-driven motor ... that powers the bacterial flagellum – a propeller-like device that enables bacteria to swim'. He shows that 'this motor, so small that 35,000 laid end to end would take up only 1mm, consists of some forty protein parts including a rotor, stator, bushings and a drive-shaft'. Behe argues that 'the absence of any one of these protein parts would result in complete loss of motor function. That is, the motor is *irreducibly complex*'.

Science points beyond itself

Science tells us there is more. It tells us there is meaning. But it can't tell us what the more or the meaning are. We need other maps, other views of reality, apart from science.[41] A road map can tell you how to get from A to B, but nothing about the weather, the rock types, the language, what makes people happy in A or who lives in B – other maps are required. Faith is one such map which deals with the 'more' of life: of meaning, of purpose, and of God.

Each of the 'signposts' I've mentioned from science are testimony to the wonder and power of science. They evoke a sense of awe and mystery which naturalism cannot explain.[42] Indeed, such a sense of the unknown, the mysterious, the awesome, can again bring science and faith together, rather than into conflict or divergence.

These signposts are not cast-iron proofs for a God, for a Creator, or specifically for the truth of the Christian faith. What they *do* show, however, is how science has its limits, and how science far from undermining faith or being in conflict with religion can *encourage and complement* our search for meaning. Philosophy and faith provide different answers to science, they are alternative maps and important ones.

Science and faith are not and never have been *necessarily* in conflict. There is much to be gained by putting them alongside one another. Our life and vision of reality are

---

[41] McGrath, *Inventing the Universe,* 38-39, 150-153. Extensively refers to the value of other maps of reality, and the complementary nature of science, theology and philosophy to life and to our understanding of the world.
[42] McGrath, *Dawkins' God*, 150-1.

poorer and shallower if we overlook either of them.

Science can't prove or disprove God. It shows a remarkable universe and reveals something of our own intriguing human nature. Science can't answer all the questions, we need other fields of life and thought for that. But both the science and the many unanswered questions of meaning point beyond themselves to something, someone, of immeasurable power, vast intellect, concerned for life, love, beauty and order, and towards whom we seem wired to relate. You can't prove that God exists, but the evidence certainly indicates there is a God, that we were made to know and enjoy him, and this astonishing universe has his fingerprints all over it.

For many, science enhances their faith. It deepens their love of science and of God. It enriches their understanding. Science answers some big questions, but can't answer many of the most important that are central to being human. What about Christian faith?

Christian faith is an act of trust, a response to the person and message of Jesus Christ. He's the foundation of Christianity – a historical reality in his person, life, death and resurrection. It is not a blind feeling, a religious frame of mind, or irrational superstition. This is not merely about ideas or morality; there is concrete evidence and a coherent message. Such a faith is an eminently *reasonable* faith. And it offers very comprehensive, rich, compelling answers and evidence for the biggest questions.

This same intelligence, reason and rationality also applies to science. Reason and rationality are not just for the scientists, but we should expect no less of them.

G. K. Chesterton states: 'The best way to see if a coat fits is not to measure the coat and measure the man, but to try it on.'

So it is with faith. Try it on, and you may find it answers many more big questions than you expect.

Discussion starter questions

1) Why do people view science and faith as 'opposing sides'?

2) Would we expect a God to be interested in science?

3) If we cannot prove there is a God then why would we assume there isn't a God?

4) We are only a collection of atoms, our thoughts are merely random firings of neurons, and we can only understand life in this context. Do you agree? How could you know?

5) Given the apparent fine tuning of the universe that allows intelligent life to exist, does this point to a creator who designed the universe to support life, or is it just outrageous, improbable luck?

Chapter 8

How can a good God allow suffering?

The Very Short Version
The material here covers a lot of ground and you might want to keep to this script or pick and choose for a shorter talk. The outline of our talk is as follows:

- Recognise that this is a huge, important, potentially personal topic.
- **Our broken world**: outline the nature of suffering, including man-made suffering (war, genocide, other types through neglect, greed, corruption, ignorance), and natural disasters. Our track record of causing suffering is plain to see. The Bible acknowledges this, faces it honestly, and Christians experience it, too.
- **How can we respond?** Christianity responds by acknowledging suffering, not denying or ignoring it, and points us to God's compassion, justice, mercy. Also, the message of the cross where God experienced suffering himself. He is with us in suffering.
- **What might God say?** The charge against God and how natural this is, but is it just? Suffering was not his plan, but we are given real freedom and make real choices. We can still turn to him.
- **The problem of suffering (and evil) if there is no God**: how, then, do we make sense of it? The invitation to trust God, even in suffering.

...

Today's Big Question is this: how *can* God allow suffering? How could a _good_ God allow suffering?[43] Or perhaps: why doesn't he fix it?

The two big questions we've looked at previously ("Is there a God?" and "Science vs faith: is God irrelevant?") are good questions, but perhaps for you they are just intellectually interesting. You *think* about them but don't *feel* the impact. Tonight's topic is one you perhaps feel the impact of very strongly. I do.

For some people, this one is a 'showstopper': any and every religion, not just Christianity, must be a lie, or pointless, or even evil, to even *begin* to think that God is worth following, given the messed-up state of the world or the loss they have experienced. For some people, suffering has transformed, even defined their lives – that 'event' they recall has shaped their entire life.

As a result, many people reject God out of hand, without much more thought. Maybe that's you, or someone you know. That's exactly why we included this Big Question in our line-up, to tackle it together. If you feel this way, you may have never stopped to think about it and I hope we can be willing to do that tonight.

This is a **huge** topic, and one that great minds have wrestled with for thousands of years, people far wiser than me! But clearly it has not stopped billions of people finding they *can* know and trust God (the God of the Bible) in the face of real suffering, and they can't all be stupid or naïve. So let's look into it, and I hope to give you some food for thought.

---

[43] We also gave this talk with the title 'Broken world: how can God allow suffering?'

There are four sections to this talk:

1) We'll look at **the nature or problem of suffering** and ask if it's God's fault.
2) We'll consider **our options in responding to suffering**.
3) **What God might have to say?** (it's only fair we let him respond!)
4) ... and **a 4th, final** reflection on this topic.

The problem of suffering: this broken world

We're talking about a reality, not theory: there is suffering and pain; evil things are done; tragedy happens. These are realities. And we feel it, and feel it is WRONG. (Take note – where does this sense of 'wrongness' even come from?) The nature of the suffering varies, and certainly in my home town of affluent Ampthill some concerns are less obvious.

These are also difficult, unpleasant realities. At times, suffering can completely dominate our lives. Or perhaps we just see it remotely on screens.

Suffering and evil can also be very significant obstacles for some people in wanting anything to do with religion or God, as they ask: *Why could this happen? Is faith just a cop-out from real life?* As though faith is simply a crutch to blank out pain, sadness or a sense of meaninglessness. I've heard that and appreciate how that feels too.

Suffering and evil are probably the greatest 'roadblock' to people taking Christianity or the Bible seriously, or to accepting a place for God in our lives at all.

Let's ask: **Where do we see suffering in the world?**

Firstly,

Man-made disasters:

[1] War: mass death, tens of millions in the 20th Century alone. The gigadeaths of two World Wars, countless other wars; death and misery on a monumental scale.

[2] Genocide: These are caused by *human* evil. I think you are hard pushed to believe there is no such thing as evil when you consider the last 100 years. The worst crimes of the 20th Century were committed by evil people and explicitly anti-religious people. Hitler (Germany), Stalin (Russia), Mao (China), and Pol Pot (Cambodia) – **just 4 men** responsible for perhaps **100 million deaths** between them. *100 million!* And that's a conservative estimate. I think it takes a certain blindness to point to God and say '**you** did that?' And genocide continues to plague our species – the Balkans, Rwanda, South Sudan, Myanmar. When will we stop?

[3] Other man-made suffering: e.g. ethnic cleansing, terrorism, child abuse, industrial and medical negligence, mass shootings in schools, domestic violence, etc.

It is a broken world, and *we* seem to be the major problem!

Secondly,

Natural disasters:

Tsunamis, earthquakes, volcanoes, floods, etc. We could also include the effects of famine which have killed millions in Africa and Asia.

But when is a natural *event* a natural *disaster*?

- A tsunami in the middle of the ocean is just *a big wave*.
- The tsunami which struck low-lying coastal areas of Asia on Boxing Day 2004, some heavily populated poor countries: 230,000 people died, 5 million affected. It was *a natural disaster*.

The difference? **Death**. That's what we find hard to face, not the physical event but the death toll. And rightly so.

Bear in mind that the numbers killed in these natural disasters are *dwarfed* by the death toll of wars and genocide, by human beings killing one another. And, in each of these 'natural disasters', we need to consider the *human culpability* for the suffering and death which followed them: e.g.

- in China and Iran, where governments ignored the need for **safe buildings**, earthquakes killed 20-30,000 at a stroke. A similar-sized earthquake in America killed 10 people.
- in Indonesia, lack of basic protection of harbours by **greedy governments** turns a survivable tsunami into an economic and human catastrophe;
- in Bangladesh, **deforestation** turns heavy rains into catastrophic flooding and lethal mudslides;
- in Ethiopia and Sudan, **political instability, corruption and civil strife** lead to millions dying of famine;
- the natural disaster of the **AIDS epidemic** in southern Africa, which claims millions each year, would be dramatically *reduced, even eradicated* if governments took action to counter the wicked myths surrounding AIDS, and invested in education

and healthcare rather than weapons, status and the personal gain within corrupt regimes.

Again and again, the toll of suffering is dramatically higher through human indifference, greed, wickedness, selfishness. Suffering is often caused by human beings. We often turn what are natural *events* into natural *disasters*.

As a purely logical conclusion, not even as a faith statement, we should stop to think before we present any charges against **God**, given **our** record. I suggest we should be slower and more humble before we start pointing the finger of blame; ask who *causes* suffering, before we demand to know why God *allows* it.

However, mercifully, you and I have probably not endured wars, we've not seen our home obliterated by an earthquake or barrel-bomb, or experienced true famine. These disasters are real, but not close to home. It doesn't remove the question, but it can be more 'theoretical' in our comfort zone.

But there are areas of our lives where pain and suffering are certainly not theoretical but very personal. There are some realities which affect **us**: chronic illness, bereavement, even tragedy (the sudden loss of a loved one), emotional hurts (the impact of other people's words, attitudes, actions), mental health issues (often unseen yet no less difficult), relational pain and suffering (the breakdown of relationships, loss of trust, abuse), gossip, slander, bullying and much more.

These are not theoretical issues. They are deeply personal and real. I have experienced several of these myself. Also, in my role as a pastor, I have encountered every one of these in the lives of others. I am not for a moment minimizing how profoundly these things can impact us.

Our question is: ***how can God allow these things?***

We'll come to what God says in minute. But if you read the Bible, you will find that it does not duck or ignore these matters. If Christianity was a cop-out, you would expect it to ignore these hard realities, but it doesn't. It addresses the reality of pain and suffering in all our lives.

Someone put it like this: 'real Christianity is so psychologically healthy. It faces reality.' So we should expect God to have a view on human suffering, as it's plainly real.

And notice, these realities also impact on Christians. They can be a profound struggle for Christians as much as non-Christians. Nowhere does the Bible suggest that in this life a follower of Jesus has some kind of immunity from trouble, a 'spiritual airbag' which inflates to protect us from life's blows.

In fact, most of the Bible's major characters faced real suffering and took their complaints straight to God: Moses, king David, prophets like Elijah and Jeremiah, Job (who is the focus of a whole book of the Bible about suffering and "why?"). Even Jesus cried out against it. Crying out to God over suffering is natural, reasonable. But there's crying *to him* or raging *against him* – two very different attitudes.

My point here is that it is a painful world, and much of the worst suffering is caused by human action before we bring God into the equation. And when we do, we find

Christianity faces this reality openly. So how does God answer this issue?

Clearly, just because *I'm* convinced that I can trust God in the face of suffering, doesn't mean *you* have to be convinced. That's fine. I would just ask you to think it through; discuss and explore the question.

So that's part 1: suffering is a reality, the world is a mess. A lot is directly our fault, through human action or negligence. We can't simply or completely lay the blame for it all at God's door.

That brings us to the next question:

What are our options in responding to suffering?

1st option (adopted by Eastern, mystical religions): **Denial** – suffering doesn't exist, it's a state of mind, or it is to be absorbed through inner peace, by focusing on yourself. Shut it out, deny it. It might work, for a while, or at times, but it's not helpful as suffering *is* real!

2nd option (typical of the Western secular, materialist mindset, with no belief in God at all): **Avoidance** – cover up suffering as a problem we don't have or 'it's somewhere else'; don't talk about it, push it out of mind, deal with it through distraction and pleasure. Avoidance just ignores the problem in another way, ignores why the world is a mess, or why we are. It doesn't dwell on suffering for long, which is good, but it doesn't want to think about it at all, which is not so healthy or helpful.

I'm not going to consider the option of 'karma' – that suffering is somehow your fault, payback for a previous life.

But there is **a better and third option**: to **face reality**, that there is suffering, and in Christianity we find a unique take on it – that God knows it, has experienced it, and gives us hope in the midst of it. In the end he has his own response.

This facing the reality involves admitting that, somewhere along the line, we are also capable of causing suffering. You and I were not responsible for the Holocaust, for tsunamis, for terminal illness in loved ones, but we still cause grief, hurt and – yes – some people do cause death, pain and untold misery. Some stir up genocide, some are bullies or liars, some break promises, trust, or bones. None of us goes through life without hurting other people – accidentally or deliberately, emotionally and physically. We can't fully deny or avoid suffering as part of the problem is that **we** are not wholly good, wise, kind or selfless ourselves. We can mess up our own lives, never mind other people's.

The Christian message faces this honest reality: we are part of the problem in a broken world, and there is such a thing as evil.

If we admit that at some level we are part of the problem, the answer could be that God could simply eliminate us all. As a matter of pure logic and even justice, that would be an answer. Eliminate the Hitlers and Stalins, the child abusers and terrorists, ... but where does it stop? To stop all suffering, all wrongdoing at every level, God would need to wipe out *everyone*. But he hasn't. That tells us something of what he is like, too.

So what *has* he done, whilst still allowing suffering in this world?

The clear answer of Christianity is this: God came, he entered this broken world, and then died to rescue and restore it. Jesus Christ died to defeat evil and offer new life, pointing to a future hope without suffering.

Christians believe the following: Jesus, God in person, lived a life as a human being and knew his fair share of heartache in his life. Jesus did not float through life on a cloud. Then he went to his death, executed on a cross, in our place.

So when we speak of pain and suffering and what God might think about this, the Christian answer points to **the cross**, the place where Jesus died. It says that there, in that event, God identifies evil as wrong and acted to defeat it. He *experienced* evil and suffering at their worst, overcame evil's power, even overcoming death, so he offers a future hope of new life as it should be.

He made it clear that his own death was not pointless suffering or a grand gesture of heroic love, but rather he acted on our behalf, dying for our sins. The Bible recounts the terrible experience of Jesus: betrayed by a trusted friend, abandoned by his followers, arrested and beaten, mocked, falsely accused, flogged. Public and painful humiliation at every point. Then the lowest point of all: he was crucified on a Roman cross. Nailed, hung, humiliated. That's profound physical, emotional and psychological suffering.

It was also the most profound *spiritual* suffering, to experience the weight of the shame and guilt of all the world's wrongdoings.

I'm not asking you to accept that. I am explaining what Christians believe. We believe this was no ordinary man, no ordinary death, but God as a man dying for us.

If that is true, this shows us a God who is *not* removed and distant from human experience, from suffering and heartache. He lived amongst hurting humanity, as one of us. He was familiar with suffering, grief, hurt and loss. The cross shows us the degree to which he entered into our human condition and experienced suffering to a measure well beyond anything you or I can fully comprehend.

Here's a God who **really is with us**, in our hurts and tears, more than perhaps we can possibly imagine. The cross shows God is loving (he died for us, in our place), God knows (he knows suffering), and God is powerful and just (through his suffering and death, he defeated evil).

If God did that, suffering should not drive us *from* God but cause us to turn *to* him. He knows what it's like. We can still ask why he *allows* suffering and we still feel it, but the same God offers us hope in our suffering and beyond it.

Which brings us to part 3:

Was this broken world God's plan? What would God say?

To help me answer this let me quote Stephen Fry, who tackled this same Big Question in an interview in February 2015 – very helpful for us! He said he would ask God why kids die of cancer, and *how could God allow that?!* He described God as 'evil, mean, capricious, and stupid'. Perhaps you think he has a point.

We need humility. We don't have an answer why specific

individual cases of suffering occur. For illnesses and accidents, typically no one can explain 'why them'. On the whole, if we claimed we did know, we've assumed God's place and that's quite an arrogant assumption.

The Christian author and activist, Krish Kandiah responded to Stephen Fry like this:

> At the heart of the Fry's argument is the idea that the world that exists is as God intended it to be. He assumes that God deliberately created a universe with appalling undeserved suffering. But a central doctrine of the Christian faith is that God created a good and perfect world and after the fall of humanity nothing is fully as it should be. To blame God for natural disasters and childhood cancer is like blaming the landlord after tenants have trashed their house.
>
> According to the Christian faith, this world is not as God intends it to be. But rather than abandoning us when we messed up, God stepped into our history. Jesus lived a life of love and grace, and died on the cross to bring forgiveness and reconciliation. He promises a future where evil is finally overthrown. The job of Christians in the meantime in our broken world is to follow in the footsteps of Jesus, showing the same love and grace to everyone.[44]

The Christian answer to suffering, is not to run *from* God, but to look *to* God, who offers real comfort and even life beyond death, the friendship of God which Jesus invites

---

[44] The full article and response from Krish Kandiah can be found at Christian Today, published 01.02.15.
https://www.christiantoday.com/article/stephen-fry-says-god-is-capricious-mean-minded-stupid-but-lets-not-get-angry/47174.htm

us to know even in the sorrows of this life.

He created a good and perfect world, with no suffering or sickness or pain, but human rebellion against his plan led to a broken world in which people choose and do bad things. Our very bodies are subject to decay and illness when that was not God's plan. The world as a whole is a violent and decaying world when this, too, was not his plan.

He didn't make us evil or damaged. But God gives people real freedom to make real decisions. We have the freedom to choose to live God's way, or not. God did not create us as robots, as automatons. He made us as people with true freedom and real responsibility. Yet we still make bad choices and some people make sinister, wicked choices. From destroying someone's childhood, someone's marriage, to someone's nation – these are the result of God making real people not robots. But it is not *his* fault what *we* choose.

A silly example: I *know* my children like ice cream and chocolate. If I ask what they want to eat after a meal (or even instead of a meal!), I know they will choose ice cream or chocolate. Have I programmed them? Is it mind-control? Is it my fault? No. It is their choice, but I *know* what they will choose. In a far greater way, *God knows* what we will choose. And we remain responsible for our choices.

It is our freedom he allows us to exercise even though our freedom can bring us conflict and pain, just as it brought all sin and sickness into the world. Even the good things we can put to damaging use: with our words we encourage or destroy people; with our technology we heal diseases and also develop weapons of mass destruction. We are moral beings, making moral choices.

We have a great capacity for goodness and kindness, but human history and culture show our capacity for evil, violence and selfishness, too. Humanity can be admirably generous and appallingly cruel.

So when we ask 'how can God allow it?' and hope he will intervene, God's clear answer is three-fold:

1) He has provided *an ultimate future hope,* through Jesus death, to deal with our wrongs and one day he will remake this world with no more suffering.
2) All evil and wrongdoing will face his *future judgement.* We rightly expect God to be just.
3) In the here and now, *he can be with us in our suffering.* Sometimes he intervenes to heal and restore. He can comfort and bring peace, if we ask. That is the experience of countless Christians around the world. He is not indifferent.

He could just leave us to it, yet he doesn't and invites our response.

There is a fourth and final aspect to this great Big Question, as we close:

The problem of suffering *without* God

Perhaps you've taken all this on-board so far and think, "It's rubbish; no God could allow such a broken world". So consider this: if we overlook the answer of Jesus and the message of the cross for the moment, we are left with an explanation in which we have to *leave God out of the picture.* A world where suffering just ... is.

Here is the world of rigid, clinical atheism:

> 'In a universe of electrons and selfish genes, blind physical forces and genetic replication, some people are going to get hurt, other people are going to get lucky, and you won't find any rhyme or reason in it, nor any justice. The universe that we observe has precisely the properties we should expect if there is, at bottom, no design, no purpose, no evil, no good, *nothing but pitiless indifference.*'[45]

I invite you to stand at the graveside of someone you love, and declare over them: you just got unlucky, blind physical forces did this in a pointless and pitilessly indifferent world.

For some, a lack of ultimate meaning does offer some kind of comfort in the face of death or suffering, which is a good thing. But for me, and billions like me, that is a profoundly unsatisfactory answer. Intellectually and emotionally, a meaningless life doesn't add up at all. The notion of a personal God who could know us, lived amongst us and even shared our suffering is far, far more satisfying, not just emotionally but also intellectually.

One other reflection on facing a world without God comes from a Holocaust survivor:

> If we held 1 minute of silence for every victim of the Holocaust then we would be silent for eleven and a half years.' So tweeted @therealbanksy in January on the 70th anniversary of the liberation of Auschwitz.

---

[45] Richard Dawkins, *River Out of Eden, A Darwinian View of Life* (HarperCollins, 1996), 133.

... millions of men, women, and children were murdered with planned and systematic efficiency.
... There are some experiences of evil before which we defend our faith only with deep sensitivity.

Elie Wiesel survived Auschwitz. He describes in painful and graphic detail his first viewing of a hanging, a young boy who stole mouldy bread, with the haunting question of the man behind him, **'Where is God now?'**.

Years later, Wiesel affirmed: 'For a Jew to *believe in God* is good. For a Jew to *protest against God* is still good. But simply to *ignore* God, that is not good. Anger, yes. Protest, yes. Affirmation, yes. But indifference to God, no. You can be a Jew with God; you can be a Jew against God; but not without God.' For Wiesel, the consequences of leaving God out of the Holocaust are worse than keeping him in.[46]

As I said at the start, we feel suffering is *wrong*. We all do and should do. Without God, where does that sense of wrongness and the hope for something better come from? Without God, we certainly can't blame him for wrongdoing and evil, and still need to ask what is wrong in our nature.

I hope all this points us away from simplistic answers that say 'God's mean and stupid' without thinking more deeply. The Bible is full of honesty and reality, and squares up to our protests. It includes plenty of people who are suffering and are no less honest with God about that, either. The Bible avoids empty platitudes and I hope

---

[46] Antony Billington, 'Not Without God', from London Institute for Contemporary Christianity's *Connecting with Culture* series, 30.01.15, licc.org.uk

I have too.

The Bible presents suffering with honesty before a compassionate God, immensely powerful yet intensely personal, great yet humble, awesome yet gentle, who knows that we live, hurt, suffer and die. It tells us that God can be trusted *even in the face of suffering, pain and evil*, perhaps especially there. Even in death's shadow, we can know him with us, if we are open to him.

Suffering doesn't mean God doesn't exist, doesn't care, or there is no hope. If anything, a Christian view of reality – rather than denying or ignoring suffering – is a more real, coherent and even honest answer.

Making sense of suffering without God is bleak and lacks a rational, satisfying argument. We want to suggest that though the world is broken, there is a God who made it and one day will re-make it – undoing the pain and sorrow and even now invites us to know him. It's not the end of our questions, but it brings real *hope*, which is a powerful human instinct. We might well ask where that comes from.

Discussion starter questions

1. Why do we think 'suffering' is so wrong, so objectionable?

2. What does it say about human beings that we cause so much suffering?

3. If there is a God, what would you expect him to do about suffering, evil, illness and death?

4. What difference might it make if God experienced this 'broken world', and knew what it is to suffer?

5. Do you think this 'broken world' proves there is no God, or he doesn't care? Why?

6. How has tonight's talk challenged, intrigued or helped you?

Chapter 9

Is Christianity just a moral myth?

The Very Short Version
The material here covers a lot of ground and you might want to keep to this script or pick and choose for a shorter talk. The outline of our talk is as follows:

- Recognise the familiar ways people view Christianity negatively.
- Highlight **the central place of the Bible to Christianity**, and how people view this – irrelevant, corrupt, nonsense. Address these claims.
- Brief explanation of **what the Bible is** – God's inspired words, a unified 'library' with various authors and genres, addressing broad and richly meaningful themes.
- Present textual evidence for the Bible as **authentic and historical**, i.e. it is a trustworthy record.
- **But is it true?** Illustrate the external evidence (secular historians, archaeology) and internal evidence (eye-witness claims, miracles, sometimes embarrassing nature of lead characters' testimony, the character of Jesus, the resurrection). And finally, it works – it changes lives!
- Conclude with **the implications** and invite a response.

...

This is a very live question to ask, in that a lot of people would have an opinion on the topic, even a very strong opinion. Let me ask you this: if you read a newspaper online and come across an article which either touches on *Christianity*, or in particular draws attention to where someone from 'the church' expresses an opinion, have you noticed that these kind of articles never fail to generate huge amounts of public comment?

And on-line public comments tend to be far noisier, more outrageous, outspoken and plain ruder than people would tend to behave in normal life. At least, I hope so, otherwise there's a lot of seriously angry people out there.

The news story might be about the church, or Christian views on marriage, money, sex, family, tax, poverty, war, government, childcare, the arms race, famine relief, or any number of other things. Whatever the story, very often you will find a response along these lines:

'Why should we take any notice of people who believe in a god in the sky?',

or, 'Who cares about these idiots who follow Bronze Age religion?'

Those are two actual quotes. I didn't make them up. And there are literally thousands like them, new ones every week.

As a side-note, I think it's interesting to notice that the church/Christians do actually have thoughtful views on such a wide range of issues, not just on 'religion' or 'the Bible'. That should tell us that they (we) aren't complete idiots. We are actually thinking about and engaged in real life, even if our opinions aren't shared!

The assertion behind these imaginative and colourful labels, without any evidence, is that **Christianity is just nonsense. It's a myth.** It's all make-believe, mumbo jumbo, a fairy tale to help the weak-minded get through life, or for the religious to fill their time doing religious things, for people of a certain personality trait, but it is certainly **not true, trustworthy, real, reasonable or relevant**.

Many would respect it, however. Many find the morality of Christian belief helpful, honourable even. Perhaps think about those individual Christians you know: do they strike you as relatively moral people? Do they strike you as fools? (Not that Christianity means you are necessarily any more or less moral or gullible than the next person, whether they have a faith or not.)

The Big Question I want to explore with you is this: even if Christianity has a *moral value* (the place of forgiveness, kindness to strangers, concern for the weak, importance of truth, etc.), is it still, basically, *just a myth?* Is it little more than a fairy story?!

What possible reasons have we for thinking that Christianity is *not* nonsense, that actually there are *reasonable grounds for faith*, such as a historical reality to this Christian belief and story?[47]

We looked at the 'God-question' in week 1, why belief in a God is reasonable. This week is specifically about Christianity, the God whom Christians claim to know and follow. The evidence, the grounds for *reasonable* faith, are inextricably linked to what we make of this book: **the Bible**. Christianity is bound up with this book.

---

[47] We gave this talk under different titles, including "Holy nonsense: Is Christianity just a myth?". Other options include "Is Christianity based on a fairy tale?", "Can Christianity be trusted?" or depending on the audience "Is the Bible trustworthy?"

- Is Christianity real, true and trustworthy? Is it all a myth? Whether you *like* the myth is a good question, but a different question. But if it's all made-up, who cares whether we like it or not?
- However, if the Bible **is** true and trustworthy, and therefore tells us what God is like and what he says to us, then each of us has to ask 'what are we going to do about that?'

There are 3 common claims raised to dismiss the Bible:

- The Bible is **irrelevant** as it's really old and about strange ancient stuff.
- The Bible is **corrupt,** it's full of contradictions and has been endlessly revised over the centuries, so you can't trust it.
- The Bible is **nonsense,** it's all made up, a myth or nice moral story in places, but not true.

You've probably heard and may believe one or more of these.

The first objection: it's **irrelevant** as it is *so* old. Let me ask you if you think gravity is irrelevant? Or love? Or antibiotics? But they're all "old". You see, whether something is relevant is a matter of whether it applies to our day, to our needs, not whether it has been around a long time. C.S. Lewis called this view "chronological snobbery" – dismissing ideas on the basis of antiquity. The Bible is old, but if it addresses unchanging human needs and nature, and our questions, it is extremely relevant.

The second common claim is that the Bible is **corrupt** – full of contradictions, a cumulative chain of compounded errors over the centuries of translation. This is a very old claim (so maybe we should immediately decide it's irrelevant!). But where are these contradictions? Where is the evidence? As for a chain of translation errors, that misunderstands or misrepresents how we get to a modern-day Bible. The Bible in English, for example, is the product of generations of experience of translation, but only one actual step of translation – from the original languages into English. Not from translation 1, to 2, to 3, and so on up to version 500 or more. It's an old claim, but where is the **evidence**?

Finally, what of the third claim that it's all **nonsense**, hocus pocus. Is it a ridiculous belief?

Think about **belief** for a moment (we also mentioned this in week 1). I wonder if you believe in the Tooth Fairy and Father Christmas? My guess is that almost every child in the Western world has done. However, these are beliefs which we grow *out of* as we grow up. We grow up, gain more understanding, become more thoughtful and we see the evidence of life around us. The evidence does not support the *existence* of these things, much less their *significance* for our life. They are well-meaning nonsense.

My grandparents lived in the Isle of Man, a beautiful island in the middle of the Irish Sea. My granny believed in the fairies who lived under Fairy Bridge. There is an actual place called Fairy Bridge! As a child I used to slide off the back seat and hide from the fairies on the floor of the car as we drove over the bridge (partly just to amuse granny, to be honest, as obviously fairies can see through cars.)

But I grew up and realised that there was no shred of *evidence* for the existence of fairies and even if there was they made *no significant difference* to my life or the universe. So I ditched that belief, aged 8 years old or so.

Like the Manx fairies, the Tooth Fairy and Father Christmas are myths that we *grow out of* as we grow up. By contrast, Christianity is a belief that people *grow into* as they grow up and as we think more deeply. Christianity bears more serious thought, not less. That's one reason we wanted to run this event. We want to be thinking about the Big Questions and show how Christianity is worth exploring more. It can also cope with robust challenges and questions.

All three objections lack evidence. We need to ask this question: **why believe Christianity is true**? And the core evidence for us to examine is found here: **the Bible**.

Other religions have their holy books: the Book of Mormon, the Koran, the Hindu writings, and so on. They claim to be *dictated* by God, angels, gods or the like with a human scribe taking down a dictation, simply recording the divine words. Other sacred writings make lesser claims. The Bible claims something very different: not dictated, but *inspired* by God. It was compiled by *people* recording historical events, writing letters, codifying their laws, composing songs, relaying sermons and speeches, yet at the same time depicting *God's* divine activity, purposes, commands, and even his intervention in person – as Jesus Christ.

You don't have to agree with that view. However, it is helpful to know how Christians understand what the Bible is. The human authors are involved but these are *God's words* with his authority and message behind them and in them.

Consider these analogies: we credit Elon Musk with putting a sports car in space, but did *he* actually build the rocket, cut the metal plates, install the engines? We would say Sir Christopher Wren built St Paul's cathedral, but did *he* actually lay the bricks and carve the stonework? We might well applaud William Wilberforce for the abolition of slavery in the 18th Century, or Florence Nightingale for a revolution in nursing care. But in all these cases other people did the work to make their ideas effective, *many different people*. In each case, however, there was *one* inspirational voice, design, purpose behind what happened. With the Bible, we recognise many different writers, but one **inspiration** behind it: one Author, Designer, Architect, Engineer, Songwriter behind all things and behind this book – **God**.

Christians see the Bible as both a *human* and a *divine* book, God's own word, believing that God speaks and actually acts through it to shape, teach, challenge and change people. It reveals God's character, not just human history or ideas. It's a purposeful book, a powerful book, a personal book – indeed far more than just a book.

But I'm jumping ahead a bit there. Let's ask the most obvious question:

What is the Bible?

- It's actually 66 books, a *library* of books. By more than 40 different authors. It includes various genres: songs, law books, history, stories, letters, prayers and short proverbs. And a four-volume biography of Jesus – the gospels.

- It addresses *vast and important topics*: human life and death, God and how to know him, where we came from, how to live, why we are here, where we are going, and all things in between including money, integrity, sex, faith, family life, forgiveness, work, honesty, love, anger, joy, our fears and our questions. Every human experience and emotion, all our hopes and needs. It's all here.

- It arose out of *different cultures and nations*. It was written over a time span of around 1500 years and was composed in 3 languages (Hebrew, Aramaic and Greek).

And yet for all that vast variety of authors, context and so on, it retains an extraordinary continuity of message and theme. The essential core message remains astonishingly consistent across the history, cultures and regions it comes from. It remains coherent across the various styles of writing in the 'library' of books, across the multiple situations and needs it addresses. A consistent message of what God is like, who we are in relation to him and what God wants for us. That isn't a *faith* statement, that's simply what you find when you study the Bible.

It is an astonishing book, whether you believe it is true and trustworthy or not. It's the most successful literary creation ever, more influential than Shakespeare or any other great text. Shakespeare has been translated into 60 languages, the Bible into well over *two thousand* – ten times more than any other book. In many languages, the Bible is the *only* book in that language. It remains the world's bestseller.

Over the past 2000 years, the Church has changed, split and fought amongst itself (sometimes about belief, sometimes for ridiculous reasons), yet the Bible has remained intact, the unchanged cornerstone document which all Christians look to and rely on.

Even if you don't believe it, it is hard to ignore its **impact**.

So that's what the Bible is.

But if it's more than just a myth, we need to ask two related questions:

1) Do we trust *the texts*? Have the manuscripts been reliably transmitted? Are these the actual original words it was meant to say? Hasn't it been 'corrupted' by now?

2) Do we trust *the content*? Even if they wrote this, is it actually true, and therefore worth believing?

Do we have the original texts?

The manuscripts which our modern Bibles come from are those related to the first section (the Old Testament) and the second section (the New Testament). Let's look at those one at a time.

The Old Testament. Written almost entirely in Hebrew, from approximately 1500BC to 400BC. By the time of Jesus (zero AD), it was essentially a set, finished set of books (actually, a collection of scrolls). But how would we know? Couldn't someone have simply tidied up any embarrassing errors and contradictions, made their own 'Old Testament' much more recently? For example, in 15th Century, when the printing press was invented, or in the 1660s when the King James Bible was produced they could have 'airbrushed' a tidier Old Testament. How do we know our version is anything like what was written and agreed more than 2000 years ago?

Good question.

In 1947, hundreds of ancient scrolls were found in some caves near the Dead Sea. They are now referred to, rather unimaginatively, as the Dead Sea Scrolls. Literally hundreds of copies of the Old Testament texts were discovered, written around *200 years BC*, thus providing a consistent picture of the Old Testament text, fitting so well with other ancient sources. The Jewish scribes who passed this book on treated it as a holy text and took great care to pass it on reliably.

What about **the New Testament**?

The New Testament is more interesting as we are dealing with a time in history which we know more about – the time of the Roman Empire – and we have far more actual source documents. It's also more important for Christianity as the historicity of the story of Jesus Christ is the very foundation of Christianity and that relies on the New Testament.

The evidence for the integrity and authenticity of the New Testament is overwhelming. Again, it is virtually undisputed by historians. Remember – this question is just about whether the text has been reliably *transmitted*, about whether it matches the original, not whether it's actually *true*.

What is that evidence for the New Testament text?

There are three factors (and you would consider all of these when looking at any ancient document):

1) The **age** of the documents (and how big is **the gap** between their age and the events they describe).

2) The **number** of documents (how many copies).

3) The **geographical spread** of the documents (where they come from).

Let's begin with the first two criteria: **the age of the New Testament documents** (and hence the gap from actual events), and **the number of copies** we have.

We can compare the Bible with the most famous classical or ancient texts:[48]

- Herodotus and Thucydides were both writing in the fifth century **BC**. The earliest copy that we have is 900**AD**. That's a **1300**-year time lapse, and we have **8** copies of each.
- Tacitus wrote his *Annals of Imperial Rome;* our chief historical source for studying the Roman world in New Testament times. There's a **1000**-year gap between his writing and when the copies we have were written, and we have just **2** copies with the middle volumes missing. Yet it's a standard, accepted text.
- Caesar's *Gallic War*: a **950**-year gap, **9** or **10** copies exist.
- Livy's *Roman History*: **900**-year gap, **20** copies.

Long gaps, *few* copies, yet they are trusted by scholars as reliable, genuine, not mere fantasy.

Compare these with the New Testament: it was written between 40 and 100AD, (that's a gap of within as little as **10** years after Jesus' death) and our earliest physical evidence is from as early as 130AD; a **90** year gap, not 900 or more!

Can you remember any events from world history from 10,

---

[48] Other useful data and background is found in Paul Barnett, *Is the New Testament History?* (Monarch, 1986), 43-47.

20 or 30 years ago, *reliably*? Can you remember where you were on 9/11, back in 2001?[49] Or Nelson Mandela being freed in 1989? Or the Moon landing in 1969? (Yes, we did land several men on the Moon.) Do we believe that records of these things are credible?

Why should ancient writers not provide a reliable record of something when the gap is so small, writing *within 10 years* of the events, and with our copies of those going back to within a generation of those authors' lives? The evidence for this text is remarkable.

The closer the documents are to the events they record, the more reliable they are. As disciples died off it became so important to write down what they had seen and heard and until then had only passed on verbally. Those written records began within 10 years of the actual events of Jesus' life and death. In historical terms, 10 years is so small as to be *vanishingly* small.

It's not just the gap, look at **the number of copies**: for the New Testament, we have 5,309 Greek manuscripts, 10,000 in Latin and 9,300 others. Around **25,000** source documents! In the ancient world, a world where so few people could read or afford writing materials, that is massive circulation.

And the third factor: **geographical spread**. The documents don't just come from Jerusalem, or Israel, but from across the entire Mediterranean: Israel, Syria, Turkey, Africa and beyond. The ancient Roman empire carried this message far and wide. The amount of historical data in these documents is so staggering, and

---

[49] For a younger audience, even more recent events will need to be included.

across all the geographical areas and varied cultures the text is so consistent that it is absurd to reach any conclusion other than these are *the actual records* of what was written 2000 years ago.

Sir Frederic Kenyon, an esteemed scholar of ancient manuscripts, expressed the same conclusion:

> 'The interval then between the dates of original composition and the earliest extant evidence becomes so small as to be in fact negligible, and the last foundation for any doubt that the Scriptures have come down to us substantially as they were written has now been removed. Both the *authenticity* and the *general integrity* of the books of the New Testament may be regarded as finally established.'[50]

The near unanimous conclusion of scholars is that the New Testament is by far and away the best preserved of any ancient writing. **Its authenticity is beyond dispute**.

And our modern Bible comes from those ancient sources, not a process of Chinese whispers of translation of a translation of a translation, multiplying errors (as some have suggested).

You simply can't make it up or sustain a lie that long and wide, that originates close to the actual event with that much data in agreement. It's not practically *possible*. Nor is it *reasonable* to argue that these texts are not original. So we're left with **a reliable record** of what was first written, especially about Jesus Christ, Jesus of Nazareth.

---

[50] F.F. Bruce, *The New Testament Documents: Are They Reliable?*, sixth edition (Grand Rapids: Eerdmans, 1981), 15, citing *The Bible and Archaeology* (1940), 288-289.

Being historically accurate and reliable does not prove that these are inspired, divine revelation, the word of God. It does not prove the claims of Jesus, or his claims on our lives. But if they were *not* historically reliable, that would bring their trustworthiness into question.

Let's move on to that second key question – is it *true*?

Do we trust the content?

Is it true, and therefore worth believing? We might agree the first disciples of Jesus wrote this, but did they make it up? Is it just a myth?

We'll consider the evidence for the New Testament and start with the external evidence (from outside the Bible) and then the internal evidence (from within the Bible).

External evidence

Secular historians

No serious historian today doubts that Jesus existed. In fact, there's a great deal of evidence outside of the Bible for Jesus.[51] The eminent Roman historians Tacitus and Suetonius both refer to Jesus.

The best witness though is an important 1st Century historian, Flavius Josephus, who was Jewish (not Christian) and pro-Roman (definitely not pro-Christian). Around the time of Pontius Pilate, he wrote this:

> 'Now there was about this time **Jesus**, a wise man – if it's lawful to call him a man, for he was a doer of wonderful works, a teacher of such men as receive the truth with pleasure. He drew over to him both

---

[51] Barnett, *Is the New Testament History?*, 16-32.

many of the Jews and many of the Gentiles.'

Then he goes on to talk about the crucifixion of Jesus and his alleged resurrection.

The best ancient historians back up the Bible's central story and character.

Archaeological evidence [52]

Go and visit the British Museum! Archaeology supports the Bible in countless confirmations of people, places, dates, titles and customs mentioned within the Bible.[53] As more sites are exposed, as more data is literally unearthed, as more ancient documents are discovered, again and again the evidence *confirms the content of the Bible*, often overturning established opinions in the process. Inscriptions on stone and clay tablets, on papyri and graves, or the discovery of entire buildings or even towns confirm the Bible's content as true.

Millar Burrows, Professor of Archaeology at Yale University, concluded:

> 'On the whole ... archaeological work has unquestionably strengthened confidence in the reliability of the Scriptural record. More than one archaeologist has found his respect for the Bible increased by the experience of excavation in Palestine. Archaeology has in many cases refuted the views of modern critics.'[54]

---

[52] Bruce, *New Testament Documents*, 94-101.
[53] For a lengthy list of specific examples, see 'Archaeology and the Historical Reliability of the New Testament' by Peter Williams. www.bethinking.org/is-the-bible-reliable/archaeology-and-the-historical-reliability-of-the-new-testament
[54] Ibid.

The archaeologist William Albright confirms this:

> Discovery after discovery has established the accuracy of innumerable details, and has brought increased recognition to the value of the Bible as a source of history.[55]

The *external* evidence for the Bible's record is immense and very credible. It tells us that the Bible is trustworthy, historically reliable, true.

Let's turn to the *internal* evidence, evidence within the Bible. There are 5 strands which we will consider.

Internal evidence

[i] Eye-witness evidence

The words are written by people known to Jesus and known by his followers. This was why they were included in the New Testament, as reliable witnesses. The first readers *knew* these people.

The writer of the fourth gospel, John's gospel, consistently and repeatedly presents himself as a 'witness'. His personal integrity and his reasons for writing rely on this being a true and reliable account. If he makes things up, his claim is a sham and his gospel would be ignored as pointless. In his closing summary, he writes this:

> ... these [things] *are written that you may believe* that Jesus is the Christ, the Son of God, and that by believing you may have life in his name.
> (John 20:31)

---

[55] Ibid.

He's writing to persuade, based on what he saw and to people who knew whether he had made it up!

Luke opens his book with a similar claim to present a careful, thoughtful record based *on eye-witness accounts*. Hardly the words of a fantasist. They present careful and public evidence.

[ii] The miracles

They weren't done in secret, in a quiet corner. They were witnessed. Why make it up if the people who were there would say, "this never happened"? The disciples and the general public weren't any more gullible or less sceptical than people are now. *They* didn't believe in miracles any more than the average person does now.

Recording these as true events wasn't something they could 'get away with' 2000 years ago, unless they actually happened. The critics of Jesus in his day did not claim that miracles didn't or couldn't happen – the evidence was plain. Instead, they argued where Jesus' power came from.

There's no real question of whether the miracles occurred, only how and why. We're not meant to simply believe that they happened. Jesus himself was not interested in proving faith through miracles, like a showman; that wasn't faith at all. Rather, Jesus' concern was for us to understand their content and meaning, not merely believe in the event – the meaning was all about him. Miracles revealed God at work in history, through Jesus. The miracles were included as *evidence for faith*, but *faith in Jesus* not in the miracles themselves.

The third strand of internal evidence:

[iii] The content is often embarrassing to its leading figures

If you were making up a myth, you would depict the first followers of Jesus as wise, brave, quick-witted, with keen minds and noble goals. Like Frodo and his friends in *Lord of the Rings*. Instead, the New Testament says they were often stubborn, doubting, devious, argumentative, selfish, narrow-minded and even a bit thick!

Why say that? Unless everyone knew they had been just like that, and yet ... what they declared was true – Jesus is God revealed and come to save us. The testimony of these embarrassed witnesses has a loud ring of truth.

[iv] The character of Jesus himself

- He comes across as *a real person*, engaging with real people in all of life – eating, sleeping, walking, talking. Not some mystical superhero.
- He spoke with *remarkable wisdom, authority, insight*. His moral teaching still shapes the world and has not been improved on.
- He made the most *staggering claims* – to be the way to God, to speak for God, to offer forgiveness and eternal life with God. Ridiculous, arrogant claims if you or I made them.
- He lived and died in a remarkable manner.
- And yet the evidence of his message was *consistent* with his life, character and miracles, with changed lives everywhere he went. His character, words and deeds left an impact.

For people who were there, the evidence of **what he said** matched **what he did**.

The reason Christianity is not a myth and makes sense rests supremely on *who Jesus is*. The nub of why we trust the Bible is the person at the centre of the story: this Jesus, who makes sense of all of life, of you and me, of who we are and who God is.

The fifth and final strand of evidence is vital:

[v] The empty grave of Jesus – the resurrection

The core data to decide whether this is all a myth is found in one place, the Bible, pointing to one man, Jesus. And the main evidence for him being <u>God</u> is that he rose from the dead. You might think that's a ridiculous thing to believe, but just for a moment consider the evidence:

[1] Very few serious scholars doubt that he actually **died**, in public. Then they buried him.

[2] By the Sunday, there was no body, just **an empty tomb**. No-one doubted that then, and no-one produced a body. No corpse was produced by his enemies to dispute it. There is no shrine at the graveside, as no one thought he was still there.

[3] There were multiple **meetings and sightings** of Jesus. Witnesses who saw him, talked with him, even ate meals with him. Not just one or two people, hundreds.

[4] **His friends** were transformed in character and behaviour, from fearful and grieving to bold and joyful, all declaring Jesus had beaten death and is alive.

[5] These first followers and tens of thousands of the first generations of Christians were **willing to die based on the reality of the resurrection – a living Jesus**, ... and the church exploded into history across the ancient world within a few years.

[6] Even today, millions of Christians face death or

torture yet rejoicing in knowing Jesus **now**.

No alternative theory adequately explains these facts, except a resurrected, risen Jesus which proved his claim to be God with power over life and death. For 2000 years, no one has come up with an explanation that comes close to satisfying the *evidence* better than this: he actually rose from the dead and is alive.

The external and internal evidence you can examine yourself. There's plenty of it, too. And it all points one way. For me the evidence is very strong that this is no myth: it's historically reliable. Belief in this Jesus is reasonable.

And there's one final piece of evidence: **it works.** Christianity isn't just an intellectual idea, *it changes lives*.

The Bible *speaks* (as God speaks, in the very human medium of words). He speaks into human life and death, into our hopes and fears. He addresses real life and our deepest need for spiritual life and hope. It changes lives.
Let me illustrate. Do you 'believe' these three ideas are real and make a difference: medicine, electricity, and music?

You probably do believe they are real and effective, that:

Medicine is not just an idea; it can save your life.

Electricity is not just a theory; it is a power we practically depend on.

Music is not just sound vibrations in your ear; music can move us to joy, dancing, crying.

Christianity is not just an idea, a lifestyle or a moral code.

It affects us deeply, if we try it. Like medicine, electricity and music it can change us. It is a life-changing message of God's rescue plan, an invitation to a relationship if we are open to that. Christianity tells us of God's medicine for the soul, God's power to live even in dark times, God's rhythm for our life in the world he made. The centre of the story is good news – a God who came into history so we could know him, Jesus himself.

You can reject it as nonsense, but I suggest you have to at least accept what you are rejecting: not an opinion based on feelings, or a myth based on speculation, but based on a historical *man*, rooted in a credible and reliable *message*, and seen in *millions* of changed lives.

You could even read it for yourself.

Discussion starter questions

1. Why do some people feel something ancient must be unreliable or untrue?

2. If God had something to say, how would you expect him to communicate?

3. Sincerity is not a good measure of whether something is true. What is?

4. What makes people think that the Bible is the 'Word of God', and what does that mean?

5. What topics would you expect the Bible to include if it was the 'Word of God'?

6. Christianity stands or falls on whether Jesus rose from the dead, as a historical reality. If he didn't, what is the point of Christianity? If he did, what might that mean for us?

Chapter 10

What is the meaning of life?

The Very Short Version
The material here covers a lot of ground and you might want to keep to this script or pick and choose for a shorter talk. The outline of our talk is as follows:

- **Recap Big Questions 1-4.**
- **Do we believe there is a meaning to life?** Only two possible options: life has no meaning or it has real meaning. Explore the implications of these, how they match experience and evidence. Note how rare unbelief is, this also takes.
- **The 'God answer'**: brief summary of why it is reasonable to believe God exists. If God exists, he is very likely to connect to life's purpose or meaning. Rather than just looking for meaning in creation we can ask the Creator.
- **Are all belief options valid?** Show how views can be sincere but wrong, some are evil or deluded. There is such a thing as truth. A simple comparison of religions shows how different they are.
- **The importance of evidence**, seeking understanding and coherence. What we might make of Jesus and Christianity.
- **What God might say the meaning of life is: to know him**. Expand on this to conclude.

...

This is the fifth of the Big Questions. I hope you have enjoyed the evenings so far, we've certainly enjoyed hosting them.

Today's topic is quite a big, broad question: **'what is the meaning of life?'**[56] We live, we die, but what is it all about?! Can we even know? And there are many ways to answer it, I'm just offering one approach this evening.

Let me give a very brief recap of weeks 1 to 4, which looked at questions which for some people can seem so big that they become obstacles to the idea that there is any possible value in pursuing the notion of God, or faith, or any kind of spiritual search.

In **week 1**, we asked: **is there a God?** If there is no good reason to think there is, we don't need to think about spiritual life any further or what such a God might want. Yet the evidence of our eyes and minds leads us to think **there probably *is* a God**, so we should probably ask what we do with that conclusion.

In **week 2**, has **science** has dealt with all mystery? Will it finally answer everything? If so, religion is just for the simpletons or those who can't cope with real life; faith is a delusion. But we saw how science is limited, it can't address every question including many of the most important ones. Much of scientific discovery actually *supports* belief in a God; science and faith can helpfully complement each other.

In **week 3**, we looked at **suffering and evil.** The world is such a mess, isn't it so blindingly obvious that either God

---

[56] We also ran this evening under the heading: "Life and Death: why are we here?"

doesn't exist or he is too callous to do much about the world? I hope we gave you food for thought in considering our own role in suffering, the good news that the God of the Bible knows and cares and how he has acted *in* the mess we so often make of our lives. We considered how the death of Jesus worked to defeat evil, as God provided a rescuer from the mess: Jesus, who lived and died as one of us.

Big Question 4 addressed the evidence behind belief in the God of **the Bible**, why we aren't dealing with belief in ancient myths. Just because Christianity has ancient origins, doesn't make it an ancient fairy tale. We considered **the evidence for Christianity being historically credible**, the reasonable grounds for the Bible to be trusted, and how the evidence centres on a man called Jesus Christ who rose from the dead. Which begs the question: how would we respond to that?

Over four weeks we've used the word 'evidence' a lot. These things can be *seen, considered, read, tested*. We aren't talking about mere ideas or opinions.

Which leads us to this topic – what does any of this mean for life, death and the universe? **What is life about? Why are we here?** These questions prompt more:

Where are we going? How can we know? What is my identity, purpose, destiny? How should we live now (our values)? These questions are ancient and natural. Everyone asks them at some level. If only God could visit us and explain ...

Life and Death. Is there a meaning to life?

Let's start with that Big Question: **what is the meaning of life?** Well, what are our options?

In *The Hitchhikers Guide to the Galaxy*, Douglas Adams famously concluded that the meaning of life is ... **42**. He may be right, but how does he know? How do *we* know? Does it matter?

'Is there a meaning to life?' is actually a very simple question with only two possible answers: *yes*, there is a meaning to life, or *no*, there isn't!

If we answer 'yes', we can ask 'OK, what is it?'

But some, a very small minority in the world today and in all of human history, answer 'no'.

This 'no' option has been especially loudly declared by the self-styled 'New Atheist' movement. Their view is that life is ultimately meaningless (there is no God, no higher purpose), and some of them can be quite angrily defiant about this. It's hard to keep being angry though, towards someone who doesn't exist. But how do they know? What does the *evidence* tell them?

If there is no God, nothing and no one beyond this life and visible reality, then this is all there is and there is no ultimate meaning. We can live, do something, die, and that's it. No ultimate accountability or justice, no reward or future, no anything beyond this life. Dust to dust, ashes to ashes, with no sure or remotely certain hope of anything else at all. This is all there was, is, and ever will be.

That's the logical conclusion, *if* there is no God.

That is the world of Richard Dawkins:

> 'In a universe of electrons and selfish genes, blind physical forces and genetic replication, some people are going to get hurt, other people are going to get lucky, and you won't find any rhyme or reason in it, nor any justice. The universe that we observe has precisely the properties we should expect if there is, at bottom, no design, no purpose, no evil, no good, nothing but pitiless indifference.'[57]

However, as I said a couple of weeks ago, I invite you, in your mind's eye, to stand at the graveside of someone you love, especially a young person, and declare over them, "you just got unlucky, blind physical forces did this, in a pointless and pitilessly indifferent world, and this is the end."

For me, and billions like me, that is a profoundly unsatisfactory answer; emotionally, rationally, and theologically it's not good enough to imply that this life is all there is and that it's ultimately pointless. To believe that takes huge *faith*, and I would suggest it also flies in the face of the evidence. It also opens up a moral void which can lead to horrendous consequences – Hitler followed this line of thinking, counting lives as of no value, and look where that led.

Most people find the idea of some spiritual reality far more satisfying – intellectually and emotionally. What Christianity proposes is a God who could know our hurts, our hopes, can be part of this life and even offer us life

---

[57] Dawkins, *River Out of Eden*, 133.

beyond death, *based on the evidence.* His reality also gives our life immense value.

Which theory fits best – meaningless life or life with meaning? Consider these:
- Think of a funeral.
- Think of your family.
- Think of the richness of human experience, feelings, creativity, music and art.
- Think of the human mind, science, and the constant desire to find meaning, to make connections, even to explore spiritual reality.
- Think of the universe, the stars in the sky, or the beauty of the mountains, trees, sunsets.

Do ANY of these fit the theory that life is meaningless?!

Throughout history, in every culture and generation, human beings have been irrepressibly religious, worshipping the sun, moon, stars and trees; we worship one God or many gods, nice gods or horrible gods, noble gods or cruel gods. *Worship and connecting with a spiritual reality seems to be something we are made for.* It is only very recently, in the affluent European and North American cultures of the past century, that communal or institutional religion has been rejected, in favour of pursuing wealth and status (or is that worshipping them?) and very individualistic lifestyles. Make of that what you will, but even here in the UK people need hope and meaning, especially in the face of death.

The irony is that in the pursuit of individual happiness, the UK at least is becoming progressively more unhappy with increasing rates of mental illness in both young and old. All the freedoms that were meant to make us happy are having the opposite effect – do we stop to wonder why?

A meaningless existence? I don't think that really cuts it when you actually think about it seriously.

And even if you do answer 'no, life has no meaning', you *still* have to explain: the **universe** and where it came from, why and how it is so **fine-tuned** to life, why we have a sense of **morality** (of good and evil), and this near-universal sense of **spiritual longing**, of inner hunger, of real felt need.

The alternative is 'yes': life has a meaning. And for the past four weeks we've sought to help clear away some of the obstacles to help explore life's big questions and tried to show that there are very good, clear, sensible reasons for belief in God.

That doesn't necessarily tell us *which* God or precisely what he is like, although we've touched on that too, but when it comes to the meaning of life sooner or later a 'God answer' stands out.

4-5 billion people alive now have reached a similar conclusion. They connect 'God' to meaning and purpose to a significant degree. They might all be wrong, but we can't argue that they are *all* stupid, naïve, brainwashed or the like. We need to at least consider the 'God answer', unless we have enough faith to believe that life is meaningless. And that takes a big amount of faith, in the face of all the evidence.

The God answer

Terry Pratchett, author of the Discworld fantasy novels, died in 2015. In the universe of Discworld, he portrayed a world which was flat and rides on the back of four elephants, each stood on a giant turtle, which is stood on another turtle, and then it's turtles all the way down.

How would we know if our world was like that? People used to think it was flat and that you could sail off the edge!

How do we find out about such things, or anything? We *look, observe, measure, and think.* We have an observable reality: the world, the universe. I think the most credible answer to the universe itself points to a Creator. We touched on this in weeks 1 and 2:

- The fact it **exists** at all, and it is **beautiful**. Who said it had to be? Creation implies a Creator.

- It is **ordered**, remarkably regular and predictable; again, who put such laws in place that describe such an ordered reality? Laws suggest a Law-maker.

- And it is so **fine-tuned** for life. It is so absurdly unlikely that life should emerge, as unlikely as filling the universe with roulette gambling wheels, one on every particle in the universe, each wheel with a million divisions of red and black, putting all your chips on just one number, and ALL those quintrillions of wheels ALL hitting the jackpot. Life is *that* unlikely, it points to a highly intelligent and purposeful design, not an accident. And a design needs a Designer.

- Fourthly, the abundance of complex, **intelligent life**. The complex, meaningful data of information, such as human DNA, for example, begs an explanation. It is fantasy to think that such complex life 'evolved' by chance without a design to follow. It is stupendously improbable.

To say these things 'just happened' is so fantastically unlikely as to be farcical, it must be untrue. Some form of super-intelligent, purposeful mind and power is far more likely. That description fits God. We are driven to a 'God answer'.

The Bible points us in the same direction when it says:

> *since the creation of the world God's invisible qualities – his eternal power and divine nature – have been clearly seen, being understood from what has been made.*[58]

Or the very first words of the Bible, Genesis chapter 1, verse 1:

> *In the beginning God created the heavens and the earth.*

The existence of creation, the sense of awe, wonder and fascination at its beauty and size and complexity, should make it plain to us that there *is* such a God. This also hints at what *kind* of God: a God of power, beauty, order, bringing life.

If that's the case, that he exists and he is like this, and we are this complex, aware, shaped by our sense of morality (good and evil) and of mortality (that there is more than this life), even of spiritual needs, then surely the meaning of life must lie with this God.

---

[58] Romans 1:20

- If you wanted to know the purpose behind **a new invention** (a car, a gadget, or device), you would ask the designer, the inventor.

- If you were given **a cake as a celebration**, you wouldn't ask the cake what it was for, or analyse the ingredients, you would ask the one who made it for you, the cook.

- If you enjoy **beautiful gardens**, walking around and exploring them, you would not assume they just appeared out of thin air, or 'evolved' from the mud, would you? They were intentionally planned and created. You would assume a gardener existed and had been at work.

If we would so naturally make that link with an invention, a cake or a garden, it's reasonable to look at the universe and conclude there is a Creator and rather than looking for meaning in the universe maybe we should ask him.

We can't *prove* that's where we find life's meaning, with knowing God, but it fits the data very well indeed. In fact, it fits better than the alternative, that there is no God and therefore no meaning.

So we have 'a God answer'.

Let me ask the next question, then: are all 'God' answers the same? Or, are all belief options valid?

Are all belief options valid?

We all believe things and many of those things are probably of no real importance to anyone else (is Costa better than Starbucks, is modern art bonkers or inspirational, etc.) We can all have a view, an opinion, but ... big deal. It won't significantly shape our life.

Other things have more of an impact on how we live our life, like *our beliefs and values*.

Your beliefs and values will shape how you answer these questions:

- What's wrong with the world?
- How can I be happy? Why am I not?
- Where do we go when we die?
- What is justice?
- How should we respond to the poor in the world, to vulnerable people, to the unborn?
- What is money for?

These aren't trivial questions. What you and I believe shapes how we live our lives.

Let me give you three examples of groups of people whose beliefs *radically* shaped their way of life:

- **the Aztecs**: they routinely sacrificed people to their gods, cutting out their hearts. At the dedication of a new pyramid in 1487, between 10,000 and 80,000 people were killed in just *4 days*. And note: their beliefs were *sincere*.
- **the Nazis**, in Germany of the 1930s and 40s: they treated large parts of humanity as sub-human, including Jews, people with disabilities, twins, Gypsies, homosexuals, intellectuals and Christians. They murdered millions, many through systematic development of technology specifically for death camps. Their beliefs in natural selection and survival of the fittest were a key element of this.

- **Islamic State** (or Al Qaeda), who brutally killed anyone who disagreed with their perverse, wicked view of life, itself a very theological view albeit evil theology. Children were beheaded, women were locked away, prisoners were burned alive. They didn't hide their beliefs, they are central to their actions.

Each belief system has implications. I would reject each of their main beliefs as untrue, deeply defective, even downright evil. My guess is, you would too. There's plain evidence that there are some things that we view as wrong, unacceptable, intolerable, untrue. That should tell us that there is such a thing as **truth**, moral absolutes, not merely opinions. There is such a thing as **evil**, not merely 50 shades of grey.

Therefore, we can't simply say that every opinion is equally valid. Some things are wrong, some things are bad. It's also ridiculous to argue that every viewpoint is just as acceptable and reasonable as another. That's plainly illogical. Nor can we say that beliefs don't matter – tell that to the victims of the Aztecs or the Nazis – one group very religious, the other atheistic. Some beliefs are evil.

When it comes to the 'God question', simply saying 'any answer will do' is what leads to 'all religions are the same', or 'all paths lead to god'. They aren't the same, they don't all lead the same way and even a basic exploration of religions tells us *how fundamentally different and contradictory they are.*

Hinduism has *many* gods, Buddhists have *none*, Christians have *one* yet relate to him as three persons: Father, Son and Holy Spirit. They can't all be right.

Judaism sees Jesus Christ as a dead impostor, Christianity declares him to be the living God and our Saviour. Islam recognises Jesus as a prophet and sinless, Christianity recognises him as more – God in person, who died to rescue us from our sins. Some religions speak of death to unbelievers, Jesus uniquely said "love your enemies". It is a nonsense to say all gods, all 'God answers', are the same.

We each choose, but they are *not* all the same and *can't* all be right. Not all of them match reality. Not all of them are good. Many are sincere but sincerely wrong. Not all beliefs offer credible hope or coherent meaning.

So how do we choose?

Richard Dawkins defined faith as 'belief in the absence of evidence, even in the face of the evidence'. I don't know of any Christian, or any Muslim or Jew for that matter, or any theologian, who agrees with that. That's not faith, that's wishful thinking.

Faith in Christian terms is rooted in *understanding and evidence*, the opposite of blind faith! A living faith engages the mind, stirs the heart, shapes the will, awakens the conscience. It *seeks* evidence and *stems* from reasoned trust; it doesn't shut out those things. That is what we have been looking at over these few weeks.

So how do we choose? How do we discern the meaning of life? I suggest that we marshal the evidence. Gather it. Look, read, talk, think, listen. Then ask: which option best fits or explains the evidence. (You could even ask God to help.)

We think these five Big Questions are good questions and suggest that the answers all point towards a 'God-answer' as being the best explanation there is. More than that, the evidence points to *the Christian God* – one who is purposeful, powerful, creative and wise, who acted in history and addresses our deepest needs, based on the evidence before our minds, our eyes and our hearts.

The Bible also points us to key evidence about *what kind* of God we are talking about. He came in person as Jesus Christ. That is who God is and what he is like. He claimed he was the real deal, the only deal. That's a big claim.

I don't expect you to believe me just because I say so, but explore and engage with the big questions yourself. Ask what best fits the evidence. The Bible is that eyewitness, expert testimony, as we discussed last week, so you can check that out too. It provides a historically credible account of God's dealings with us, his message to us, his personal appeal, focused on the life and death of one man, Jesus of Nazareth.

So we can make up our minds, but the options are limited. What will we make of Christianity?

Tom Wright, a leading Christian theologian, put it like this:

> Christianity is either the most devastating disclosure of the deepest reality of the world, or it is a sham, a nonsense, a bit of deceitful playacting.[59]

The New York City pastor, Tim Keller presents our options as follows:

---

[59] N. T. Wright in Timothy Keller, *King's Cross, The Story of the World in the Life of Jesus* (Hodder and Stoughton, 2011), 45.

Jesus is either a wicked liar or a crazy person and you should have nothing to do with him, or he is who he says he is and your whole life has to revolve around him and you throw everything at his feet.[60]

Those are the options – either the greatest sham of all history, or the truth and therefore something we need to respond to. We must **examine the evidence.**

There's one final reflection on this Big Question:

What might <u>God</u> say the meaning of life is?

If he exists and is as powerful and as downright amazing as he seems to be or claims to be, and if the Bible is true and he knows we are here, then – as I've already alluded to a few times – *surely* it makes sense to think he has a view on the meaning of life. It would be bizarre to think an all-powerful, supremely intelligent, creative and purposeful Being had no further thoughts on the matter!

Here are some other perspectives on the meaning of life:

- Pleasure is everything
- Give in to happiness
- Life is fleeting, clasp it hard with both hands
- Seek delight
- Trust your impulses
- Ordinary is pointless
- Break free

That's not from the Bible. It's written on the packaging of *Gü York Cheesecake*, available in all good supermarkets.[61]

---

[60] Timothy Keller, *King's Cross,* 45.
[61] Other calorific desserts are also available.

Is that it – God has made us simply to be happy, "pleasure is everything"? Do what you want – eat, drink and be merry for tomorrow we die? Did he have nothing more to offer than this life, despite our sense that he did, despite our hopes and fears and sense of mortality? It seems unlikely.

Jesus himself described our problem as like 'hunger and thirst'. Just as we have physical appetites and needs, we can tell we are spiritually needy. He said he could satisfy that hunger, fill our emptiness, give us life, establish real hope.

The consistent message of the Bible, the message Jesus spoke of and lived by and died for, is bigger and better than 'be happy' as a meaning for life. It is, if we are being honest (whatever our thoughts on religion or Christianity) exactly what you would expect of a God whom life and the universe points to. That message, that meaning is this: *the meaning of life is to know God.* To enjoy life not just here as we are, but *here with him* and even *beyond death with him.*

The meaning of life is life with God.

A life full of experiencing him, knowing his care, following his direction, accepting his forgiveness, enjoying his friendship, having hope in him beyond death. For me, the *evidence* tells me that is what we are made for.

Life is so full of meaning. This is one reason why death is so awful, the separation from a once-living and once-loved person. That meaning is worth exploring. That inner sense of 'more' won't be filled if we ignore the God question.

If we leave God out of the picture, we are still left asking: *what is life for? where did all this come from? why do I feel there is more to life than this?* Intellectually and emotionally, we need answers. The hunger and thirst remain. If there *is* a God (and he's powerful, creative, wise, and so on), it's got to be worth pursuing that personal question: what has he got to do with me? Many have found him to be very satisfying, even for a question as big as the meaning of life.

Thanks so much for listening and for coming along. Do keep on exploring these Big Questions, and come and talk with us too.

Thank you.

Discussion starter questions

1. Do you think life has a meaning? What leads you to this conclusion?

2. What do you think of the 'God answer'?

3. What difference might it make which God or gods we choose?

4. Why do you think we sense our mortality, a need for meaning, and our spiritual need?

5. If there is a God who can meet our needs, and we can know him, how might you respond?

6. What have you got out of this event / this evening?

7. How do our views of such big questions shape how we live?

Books and Resources

There are many, many high-quality, accessible resources available offering Christian answers in apologetics. There are books and websites galore. Two particular online resources are worth highlighting for apologetics resources from an evangelical perspective: BeThinking and Stand to Reason.

BeThinking (www.bethinking.org) is provided by UCCF: The Christian Unions, the UK charity whose aim is making disciples for Jesus Christ in the student world. Their website is very easy to navigate and offers resources under the headings 'engage' (general questions about life), 'explore' (questions about Christianity; what we believe and why), 'compare' (comparing Christianity to other religions and beliefs), and 'relate' (relating the Christian faith to all of life, e.g. meaning and morality, sexuality and gender, faith and work).

Stand to Reason (www.str.org) are a US-based group led by Greg Koukl. Their mission is described as follows: "Stand to Reason trains Christians to think more clearly about their faith and to make an even-handed, incisive, yet gracious defense for classical Christianity and classical Christian values in the public square." Their website offers a wide range of resources.

Below is a list of books which we made available during Big Questions for people to browse, borrow, buy or receive as gifts. We brought with us those books listed under 'General' every week, the others were available on the relevant evenings.

General
Copies of Mark's gospel (free to all guests)
Barry Cooper and Paul Williams, *If you could ask God one question*
C.S. Lewis, *Mere Christianity*
Lee Strobel, *The Case for Christ*
Andrew Wilson, *If God, then What? Wondering aloud about truth, origins and redemption*
The Bible

Week 1 Is there a God?
Timothy Keller, *The Reason for God: Belief in an Age of Scepticism*
Keith Ward, *Why there almost certainly is a God*

Week 2 Science vs. faith: is God irrelevant?
Edgar Andrews, *Who Made God?*
Ruth Bancewicz, *God in the Lab: How science enhances faith.*
John Lennox, *God's Undertaker: Has science killed God?*
Scott Petty, *Little Black Book: Science and God*

Week 3 How can a good God allow suffering?
Scott Petty, *Little Black Book: Suffering and Evil*
Philip Yancey, *Where is God when it hurts?*

Week 4 Is Christianity just a moral myth?
Barry Cooper, *Can I really trust the Bible?*
Amy Orr-Ewing, *Why Trust the Bible? Answers to 10 tough questions*
Scott Petty, *Little Black Book: The Bible*
Scott Petty, *Little Black Book: Jesus*

Week 5 What is the meaning of life / Am I wired for a spiritual life?
John Ortberg, *When the Game is Over, It All Goes Back in the Box*
John Ortberg, *Soul Keeping, Caring for the most important part of you*
Scott Petty, *Little Black Book: What's Life All About?*
Philip Yancey, *Prayer*

Depending on the timing, we also offered publicity related to Christmas or Easter events. It also helps to have a general church contact card available and perhaps literature related to other church groups or events (Alpha, Christianity Explored, youth groups, seniors activities, children and families, etc.).

Further reading

There are countless excellent books and resources available grounded in the Bible, committed to addressing these big questions from a Christian perspective with the gospel in mind. Here I list just some books which have been helpful in terms of general background reading for preparation on these topics. This is not a definitive nor an exhaustive list, but it might be helpful depending on your interests, background, needs or resources.

The numbers **[x]** indicate which of the first four Big Questions a book might particularly relate to, although several have a wider relevance. Books without a number typically relate well to question **5**, 'the meaning of life' from a Christian perspective. Some books relate to a wide range of topics and also the nature of asking good questions in general.

I have not included the 'Little Black Book' series here, but this series aimed at young people provides very short, thoughtful primers on several of the main topics.

Denis Alexander (ed.), *Can We Be Sure About Anything? Science, Faith and Postmodernism*, IVP Apollos, 2005. **[1,2,5]** *A collection of essays, with input from theologians, scientists and philosophers.*

Edgar Andrews, *Who Made God? Searching for a theory of everything*, Evangelical Press, 2009. **[1]** *Chock-full of anecdotes and illustrations from science.*

Christopher Ash, *Where was God when that happened?*, Good Book Company, 2017. **[3]** *Principally aimed at Christians, part of the 'Questions Christians Ask' series of short books. Focused on helping Christians understand God's sovereignty and his providence.*

Ruth Bancewicz, *God in the Lab: How science enhances faith*, Monarch, 2015. **[2]**

Henri Blocher, *Evil and the Cross*, IVP Apollos, 1994. **[3]**

F.F. Bruce, *The New Testament Documents: Are They Reliable?* (6th edn.), IVP, 2000. **[4]** *Encouraging, brief, and stunningly clear.*

D.A. Carson, *How Long, O Lord? Reflections on suffering and evil*, (2nd edn.), Baker Academic, 2007. **[3]**

Francis Collins, *The Language of God: A Scientist presents Evidence for Belief*, Simon and Schuster, 2007. **[2]**

Barry Cooper, *Can I really trust the Bible? And other questions about Scripture, truth and how God speaks*, Good Book Company, 2014. **[4]** *Principally aimed at Christians, part of the 'Questions Christians Ask' series of short books.*

Paul Copan, *Is God a Moral Monster? Making sense of the Old Testament God*, Baker Books, 2011. **[3]**

Steven Croft et al. (eds.), *Evangelism in a Spiritual Age. Communicating faith in a changing culture*, Church House Publishing, 2005. *Highlights the questions our culture is asking, including that of origins and God's existence.*

Kevin DeYoung, *Taking God at His Word: Why the Bible is worth knowing, trusting and loving*, IVP, 2014. **[4]** *Short, punchy explanation of why we can trust the Bible and what that means for us.*

Timothy Keller, *The Reason for God: Belief in an Age of Scepticism*, Hodder and Stoughton, 2008. **[1]** *A modern classic, presenting clear arguments but not a light read.*

Timothy Keller, *Making Sense of God: An Invitation to the Sceptical*, Hodder and Stoughton, 2016. **[1]** *A kind of follow-up to 'Reason for God', addressing how Christianity provides a rich and satisfying source of meaning, satisfaction, freedom, identity, justice and hope.*

John C. Lennox, *God and Stephen Hawking: Whose Design is it Anyway?*, Lion, 2011. **[1,2]** A short, clear book and robust response to Hawking's *Grand Design*.

John C. Lennox, *God's Undertaker: Has Science Buried God?*, Lion, 2007. **[2]** *Insightful, comprehensive and full of lively illustrations from science to point to creation, a creator, the apparent fine-tuning of our world, and the limits of science.*

C.S. Lewis, *Mere Christianity*, HarperCollins, 2015.

C.S. Lewis, *The Problem of Pain*, HarperCollins, 2015. **[3]**

Alister McGrath, *Dawkins' God. Genes, Memes, and the Meaning of Life*, Blackwell, 2005. **[1,2,5]** *More detailed than his publication 'The Dawkins Delusion', this excellent resource provides a robust critique of Dawkins' popular book and shows where Dawkins draws his conclusions from his own scientific views, and how these fall short of valid conclusions.*

Alister McGrath, *Inventing the Universe, Why we can't stop talking about science, faith and God*, Hodder and Stoughton, 2016. **[1,2,5]** *A highly respected scientist and apologist, McGrath provides a rich exploration of how science and faith complement one another as maps of reality. A superb all-round book on apologetics.*

Mark A. Noll, *The Scandal of the Evangelical Mind*, IVP, 1994. **[2]** *Chapter 7, 'Thinking about Science', reflects on how skewed, narrow, defensive and unthinking attitudes towards science from within evangelicalism, in the US particularly, have denied Christians or Christianity the joys, riches and credibility they should enjoy. Scientific creationism is a particularly serious example of this. A brilliant and incisive book.*

Amy Orr-Ewing, *Why Trust the Bible? Answers to 10 tough questions*, IVP, 2008. **[4]** *An excellent short introduction to the contemporary challenging questions about the Bible.*

Francis Spufford, *Unapologetic: Why, despite everything, Christianity can still make surprising emotional sense*, HarperOne, 2012. *A bit sweary in places, but makes some brilliant arguments for the role, significance and reasonableness of Christianity in the UK today. Also extremely funny, and helps Christians to see how weird we must seem at times.*

Keith Ward, *Why there almost certainly is a God: Doubting Dawkins*, Lion, 2008. **[1]**

Timothy Ward, *Words of Life: Scripture as the living and active word of God*, IVP, 2009. **[4]** *See chapter 4 especially.*

Elie Wiesel, *Night*, 1958. **[3]** *Short, award winning testimony of the Holocaust.*

Paul Williams and Barry Cooper, *If You Could Ask God One Question*, Good Book Company, 2007. *A short, lively, accessible introduction to many of the most common questions and objections to Christianity.*

Andrew Wilson, *If God, then What? Wondering aloud about truth, origins and redemption*, IVP, 2012. *A superb all-round book exploring the major big questions in the title; lively and very readable.*

Jared C. Wilson, *Unparalleled, How Christianity's uniqueness makes it compelling*, Baker Books, 2016. *Clear and accessible, exploring some key doctrines of the Christian faith and how they are distinctive, with a gentle sense of fun in its tone. A good primer book on this topic. Along the way, Christianity is compared in various ways with other religions (especially Islam and Judaism), with some sects (Mormons, JWs), and with secular worldviews, without getting too technical.*

Christopher J.H. Wright, *The God I Don't Understand, Reflections on Tough Questions of Faith*, Zondervan, 2008. **[3]** *Including evil and suffering, biblical 'genocide, the cross, and the end of all things.*

N.T. Wright, *Evil and the Justice of God*, SPCK, 2006. **[3]** *Chapter 1 is especially helpful, showing how vital it is for our modern world to* *understand evil as a reality, to avoid thoughtless or immature answers or over-reactions.*

Tom Wright, *Surprised by Hope*, SPCK, 2007. **[4,5]** *On the resurrection and how this shapes our hope and Christian life now.*

Philip Yancey, *Where is God when it hurts?*, Zondervan, 1997. **[3]** *Practical, personal, pastoral. A Christian response to pain and suffering, from the Bible and personal experience, and how to support others in the midst of suffering.*

Test of Faith, www.testoffaith.com **[1,2]** *A resource from the Faraday Institute for Science and Religion. Includes a DVD with interviews with ten eminent scientists from a wide range of disciplines, each of whom share how faith relates to science.*

Big Questions

ACKNOWLEDGEMENTS

This course has only been possible to develop and deliver with the encouragement and prayers of a whole church, Ampthill Baptist Church, who also paid for the coffee. In particular, I wish to acknowledge my sincere thanks to Peter Laws, Martin Sutch, Alex Vickers and Gary Wood for helping shape the event, sharing in giving the talks, welcoming the guests, for Martin's graphic design skills, and for their consistent support which helped make this such an encouraging and enjoyable event.

ABOUT THE AUTHOR

Andrew Goldsmith is married with two children and is currently serving as Senior Pastor of Ampthill Baptist Church in Bedfordshire. The family pets are two indoor rabbits. That's right, indoor.

He has been in ministry for over 10 years with an emphasis on Bible preaching and teaching, and everyday discipleship. He also enjoys creative and lively ways to engage in apologetics (explaining and defending Christianity) and helping people connect with Jesus through the Bible.

He has been in leadership of churches in Leeds and NW London and studied at London School of Theology. Prior to pastoral church ministry he worked in industry and academia in the area of medical engineering, developing replacement hip and knee joints.

His previous book, *Formation Groups: Transforming Disciples*, is also available via Amazon.

Made in the USA
Columbia, SC
17 June 2018